Following God
for YOUNG ADULTS

W9-BNA-000

GOD IS...
Exploring The Many Sides of God

A STUDENT DEVOTIONAL GUIDE
by
David Rhodes & Chad Norris

Advancing the Ministries of the Gospel
AMG Publishers
God's Word to you is our highest calling.
CHATTANOOGA, TENNESSEE

Following God:

God is ... Student Devotional Guide

Copyright © 2003 Wayfarer Ministries, Inc.

Published by AMG Publishers.

ISBN 0-89957-732-6

First printing: May 2003
Edited by: Robert Neely and Rick Steele
Graphic design: ImageWright
Cover design: ImageWright
Special thanks to: J. Roger Davis, Linda Gilden, Chuck Wallington

Wayfarer Ministries
Box 201
1735 John B. White Sr. Boulevard
Suite 9
Spartanburg, SC 29301-5462
864-587-4985

Printed in Canada

08 07 -T- 6 5 4 3 2
web sites: www.wayfarerministries.org   www.amgpublishers.com

To Kim and Wendy:

Your sacrifice made this possible!

Table of Contents

GOD IS...

This study has a simple name; however, its goal is anything but simple. The task of describing who God is, is a monumental one. The words "God is ..." are loaded.

The question at the heart of this study is, "When I think about God, what am I thinking about?" All of us probably understand some truths about God, but most of us haven't come close to seeing the whole picture.

Discovering who God is is a tough task that becomes even more difficult when we try to make sense of the characteristics of God that seem to be at odds with each other. How can God be both huge and personal? How can he be both holy and gracious? How can he be both our Father and a jealous God? How can he be both God of the ordinary and a mysterious God?

Eugene Peterson once made the statement that discipleship is a decision to follow God based on what we **know** about him and not what we **feel** about him. As we learn to think correctly about God, our lives change.

We hope these devotions will stretch how you see God. We'll examine some of the attributes of God, paradoxes and all, and explore what they can mean in our lives and how they can change us.

Tips...
...on using this devotional book

This student devotional book is intended to help you learn about eight of the characteristics of God: about how he is both huge and personal, both holy and gracious, both jealous and our Father and both ordinary and mysterious.

Some of you are working through this study on your own, and some of you are going through this study in a group. Either way, this book is designed to take some of the truths of God's character and help you apply them to your daily life. If you are studying "God is . . ." in a group, this book is not designed as a replacement for those group sessions. Our hope is that, if you've gone through the devotions in the week leading up to your group time, you will be able to share your thoughts with the group and build on the things you learned during the week during that time. If you are going through this study on your own, we hope that you will take some time to enter into discussions with your friends, family, and ministers about the things you are learning.

The book is divided into eight lessons with the purpose of allowing the reader to do one lesson per week for eight weeks. There are five devotional readings for each week's lesson. Although we have divided the devotions according to the five-day schedule, feel free to create your own schedule for completing your study.

Recognizing that there is no perfect structure for time alone with God, we have tried to produce devotions that are both varied and consistent. This book provides stories, questions, illustrations, background information, charts, and other tools to help illuminate the featured Scripture for each day and encourage and challenge your view of God.

Finally, at the end of each week, there is a notes page, which we hope you will use to take notes during your group session if you are going through "God is . . ." with others or to journal your own personal highlights from the week if you are going through the study on your own.

We believe this study will help you grow in your understanding of God, and we hope that you will have fun in the process. Let the journey begin.

GOD IS...

HUGE

a God-sized God

GOD IS...HUGE

more than
a distant grandfather

■ When you think about God, what kind of picture comes to your mind? Try to avoid a typical Sunday School answer.

big soft clouds in the sky with a loving father sitting with open arms among them

■ What distorted pictures of God do people have today?

that he punishes you and doesn't love you unless you're a strict Christian

We're going to spend the first week of our study of who God is by looking at some of the distorted pictures of God that all of us have from time to time. Today's devotion deals with the picture of God as a distant grandfather.

I love my grandparents. They always have spare change and time to help. I can remember my grandfather taking me fishing, ordering me my first Big Mac and taking me to the store for no-holds-barred candy runs. There was nothing like going to Grandma and Grandpa's house for two or three weeks a year. The problem was that, after those two or three weeks, I had to leave Grandma and Grandpa and return home, which was ten hours away. While we kept in touch through letters and phone conversations, talking to Grandpa on the phone wasn't the same as having him wake me up early in the morning to head out on a fishing trip. My grandparents were involved in my life, but for most of the year they were involved from a distance.

Sometimes it's easy to see God as a distant grandparent, as loving and patient but far away from us. While we find comfort in his gentle acceptance, we aren't really sure he is involved in our daily lives. It's nice to hang out with him for a couple of weeks a year at summer camp or maybe over Christmas break. But as for our everyday lives, he is out of our sight and therefore often out of our minds.

Read Psalm 23

Fill in the blank:

Psalm 23:1 begins, "The Lord is my _Shepherd_."

■ How does this psalm shatter the picture of God as a distant grandfather?

it says God rules people

■ What are some differences between a distant grandfather and a shepherd?

a grandfather is boring

■ What does seeing God as a shepherd mean to your everyday life?

Most of us have heard Psalm 23 many times, and we may have even memorized it. But sometimes, the things that are easily remembered are hard to get into our real lives. To think of God as our shepherd is an earth-shattering concept. In this passage, David, who had spent plenty of time working as a shepherd, looks at his flock and sees a picture of God guiding his own life. As a shepherd, David had many times led his sheep to green pastures, protected them from prowling enemies, steadied them with his staff in dangerous situations and led them to quiet waters to drink. In this reflection, David recognizes how active God has been in his everyday life. God is not distant. He's close.

prayer exercise:

Spend a few minutes reflecting on your own life and looking at some ways that God has been a shepherd to you. Remember how he has guided and protected you in the past. Spend some time thanking him for his daily presence.

more than
a vending machine

The invention of the vending machine revolutionized the snack-food world. It's no longer necessary to drive to the convenience store for a candy bar or soft drink. Now, vending machines line the halls in many public places, waiting to cater to us. They give us the convenience of snacks on demand. Candy bars, soft drinks, crackers and even sandwiches are available as soon as we slip some spare change or a dollar bill into a machine and press a button or two. How would American students eat if vending machines hadn't been invented?

But vending machines are not always problem-free. Many of us have felt ripped off and cheated by a vending machine that left a candy bar hanging halfway out of the spiral feeder, dangling just out of reach. We can relate to being cheated by machines that took our money without giving us our soft drinks. The emotions we experience as we beat on those machines, shake them, and rock them from side to side show just how desperate for convenience we are. When we put our money in the machine, we expect to get what we want and get it now.

Many Christians see God as a giant vending machine. All too often, we come to God expecting to insert our coins and get whatever we want in an instant. We spend a day praying for something we badly want, and if God does not deliver, we get mad, showing the same impatience that we do with vending machines. We're angry that God has not catered to us at our convenience. It seems harsh to say it that way, but many times that's how we really feel. Today's passage points us in a different direction. God is more than a vending machine.

Read Matthew 6:25-34

■ How do the words of Jesus shatter the concept of God as a vending machine?

_____

_____

_____

■ What is the difference between asking God to get on our agenda and moving to get on God's agenda?

God doesn't move to ours

■ On a normal day, which of the following statements is true of you:

☐ I am on God's agenda.
☒ I try to put God on my agenda.

■ How would your life change if your perspective of God changed?

i would probably chill out about things i worry about

The words of Jesus here in Matthew 6 offer a striking contrast to the picture of God as a vending machine. Jesus tells his followers not to be so concerned about everything the world has to offer. This is a message that crosses over to Christians in our generation.

How many times do we try to use God to get everything we wanted before we met God? So often we chase after all the same things that the world chases after and simply try to use God to get us there. Jesus has a different idea. In this passage, Jesus shatters the mentality that God exists for us and leads us to the conclusion that the opposite is true: We exist for God.

Jesus is not saying that all of the things we long for are not important. He is simply saying that those things are not as important as God's things. He's saying that if someone should act like a vending machine, it's us and not God. And in his grace, God does not treat us like creations for his convenience. Jesus tells us to put our eyes on God, to seek him and to trust him to take care of our needs. It's a relationship, not a transaction of convenience. God is our Father, not a vending machine.

prayer exercise:

Many times, we spend our prayer lives asking God to give us things. This is a part of prayer, and God wants us to ask Him, but that is not all prayer is about. Spend some time today turning the tables. Ask God what he wants from you today and spend some time praising him for who he is.

more than
an angry police officer

When my sister was a senior in high school, she had an experience she will never forget. As she was driving to school one day, she pulled out in front of a car, almost causing a wreck. It was a really close call. The driver of the other car was furious, and my sister felt terrible. As she continued her drive to school, she decided to put on some lipstick. When she started to apply it, she accidentally wove in and out of her lane and almost had another wreck. The driver of the other car was furious, and my sister again felt terrible.

What my sister did not realize is that some police officers live every day of their lives on the prowl, looking to pull over bad drivers. These officers know exactly where to lie in wait, like lions ready to pounce on their prey. Nothing thrills them more than to witness someone going 54 miles per hour in a 45 m.p.h. zone. My sister was about to meet one of those officers.

As my sister kept driving to school, she noticed flashing lights behind her. She panicked as she realized she was being pulled over. Her heart pounded as she stopped on the side of the road. She was scared the policeman was going to give her a ticket.

As she looked back toward the officer, she saw a man with a furious look on his face. She knew she was in trouble. He slowly and methodically marched toward her car. When he arrived at her window, he snarled, "I can't believe how careless you've been. You're going to get yourself killed or kill someone else if you keep driving like this. I've been watching you for the last few miles, and I ought to take your license. It's drivers like you who put me over the edge."

Then the officer pulled his gun and shot my sister in the leg.

Of course, I'm just kidding about the shooting part. But he was very upset. My sister started crying and kept saying she was sorry. She ended up getting off with a warning. She was so relieved that she didn't have to take a ticket home to our parents.

Doesn't it seem odd that many of us view God as an angry police officer who has strategically placed his patrol car in a spot where he can nail us after he sees us make a mistake? God doesn't overlook our sin; however, the

Bible clearly shows us that he is not standing in heaven with a hand on his gun, ready to shoot us in the leg when we mess up. One of the greatest definitions of God in the Bible is this: **God is love.**

■ Do you have the tendency to look at God as an angry police officer who loves to catch people when they break the rules?

   ❑ yes
   ☒ no

■ Does God wander around heaven on the prowl, waiting for his children to mess up so he can pull them over and give them a ticket or even take them to jail? How do you know?

<u>Yes so he Can give them a</u>
<u>Chance to ask for forgiveness</u>

The book of Hosea shatters the picture of God as an angry police officer. The theme of this book is God's steady love for Israel despite her continued sin and unfaithfulness. Hosea married Gomer, only to discover that Gomer would not be faithful.

Despite this betrayal, God instructs Hosea to pursue her and love her again. Through this process, we see a beautiful picture of God's love for his people.

Read Hosea 3

■ Does Hosea 3 depict an angry, frustrated God? How so?

■ Describe the picture of God in Hosea 3.

_____

_____

■ What are some ways you tend to turn away from God and pursue other things as Gomer did?

_____

_____

_____

God does not overlook our sin. His only Son had to die so that people could be forgiven. Without the cross of Christ, there would be no reconciliation between God and his people. God has never treated sin lightly.

But in the mystery of his amazing grace, we find a God who continues to pursue us despite our sin. What an incredible display of love! He is not an angry police officer pursuing to punish us. He pursues us and gives us an open invitation full of love.

prayer exercise:

Spend some time reflecting on the amazing truth that God pursues us not to punish us but to love us. Tell the Father how much you are amazed by his love. Ask him to help you as you continue your spiritual journey.

GOD IS... HUGE

more than
a paramedic

September 11, 2001, is a day we will never forget. A beautiful morning quickly turned into a day that changed our country forever. Hijackers took over planes and smashed them into the World Trade Center's twin towers and the Pentagon. We had no idea the world would stop that day or that we would have to cope with such a great tragedy.

Moments before the crash, our world was a very different place. Democrats argued with Republicans. Prayer was forbidden in schools. God was on few people's minds. But for at least a few days after the crash, Republicans and Democrats stood hand in hand; schools were filled with prayer; and God was on many people's minds. This horrific attack on our country dramatically affected our view of things.

Many of us turn to God in times of crisis. The picture of God as a paramedic fits nicely with our view of God and world. We are content to seek our own things and go our own ways when life is normal. We reserve God for moments of tragedy or devastation. We don't seek God until we are in an emergency.

But when bad things happen, we frantically call 9-1-1 for God and plead that if he will help us out of our situation, we will give him the rest of our lives.

■ **What is right and what is wrong with viewing God as a paramedic?**

Right | Wrong

■ **How is God more than a paramedic?**

_____

_____

_____

■ Have you ever fallen prey to seeing God as nothing but a paramedic you call when you get in a desperate situation? Explain your answer.

Read Psalm 63

■ How does this psalm challenge the view of God as a paramedic?

Psalm 63 shows David in a 9-1-1 situation. His call to God is very intense. But in his cry to God, we find something different than a view of God as a paramedic. Verse 2 is the key. David says, "I have seen you in the sanctuary, and beheld your power and your glory." What David implies here is that he is not calling out to a stranger. He is not calling for someone he sees only when things are desperate. His cry for help goes to someone whom he knows from his day-to-day life. David has a passion and desire for God that is fascinating. He says, "Your love is better than life" (v. 3). David has decided he wants to be with God as much on his best day as he does on his worst day.

David's words are convicting. It's easy to recite the words of Psalm 63 when our lives are in shambles. It's harder when we're on top of the world and everything is going well. Thinking about God as more than a paramedic leads us to the reality that being with God is better than the best day we could have on our own.

- How does the truth that being with God is better than the best day we could have on our own challenge you in your spiritual walk?

_____

_____

_____

- Do you have a passion like David?

  ☐ yes
  ☐ no

If your answer is no, what holds you back?

_____

_____

_____

Fill in the blanks:
Take a few moments to write a psalm of your own, using the format of Psalm 63.

O God, you are my God, _____ I seek you; my body longs for you, in

_____.
I have seen you in _____ and beheld your _____ and your
_____. Because your love is better than _____, my lips will glorify you. I will praise you as long as I live, and in your name I will _____. My soul will be satisfied as with
_____; with _____ my
_____ will praise you. On my bed I remember you. I think of you _____.

Because you are my_____, I sing in the shadow of your wings. My soul _____ to you; your right hand _____ me.

They who_____ my life will be _____; they will _____.

But _____ will rejoice in God; all who swear by God's name will praise him, while the mouths of liars will be silenced.

prayer exercise:

Spend some time thinking about your best day. Then spend some time telling God that being with him is better than that best day. Read the psalm that you wrote as praise to God. Close your prayer time with a few moments of silence.

more than
a teddy bear

Girls love teddy bears. Just walk into any store around Valentine's Day or Christmas to confirm this fact. I can remember giving my girlfriend (who is now my wife) a stuffed animal when I was about to go away to graduate school for a year. We were going to be experiencing a dreaded long-distance relationship, and I wanted to give her something to remind her of me. I gave her a dog with a sock hanging from its mouth. She still has that stuffed animal.

People fall in love with stuffed animals or teddy bears for many reasons. In fact you may even have one of your own. (Guys often won't admit it, but their mothers probably have some incriminating evidence.) It's amazing how stuffed animals can bring hours of joy, excitement, and comfort.

When kids get scared, teddy bears protect them. When they are sad, teddy bears encourage them. When they feel alone, teddy bears comfort them. When they're having fun, teddy bears play with them. Teddy bears are always positive, always safe, and always ready to do whatever their owners wish.

Sometimes it's easy to think of God as a big teddy bear. For many people, that's the extent of a relationship with God. When they get scared, God, their teddy bear, protects them. When they're sad, God, their teddy bear, encourages them. When they feel alone, God, their teddy bear, comforts them. When life is going well, God, their teddy bear, shares in the fun. To them, God is always positive, always safe, and always ready to do whatever they want, almost as if they owned him.

■ Take a moment to evaluate the following statements. Some of these statements depict thoughts of God that are correct. Place a check in the boxes next to those thoughts. Other statements depict thoughts of God that are wrong. Place an "X" in the boxes next to those thoughts.

- ☐ As long as I have God, nothing bad will happen to me.
- ☐ God is always available.
- ☐ God stays beside me.
- ☐ God never gets angry.
- ☐ God encourages me.
- ☐ God does everything I want him to do when I want him to.
- ☐ God is dependable.
- ☐ God serves me.

Read Numbers 14

■ How does this passage challenge the picture of God as a teddy bear?

_____

_____

_____

_____

We don't have to go very far in life or in the Bible to find out that God is not a teddy bear all of the time. The God of the Bible resists being cornered in such a box. In Numbers 14, we find the people of Israel refusing to go into the Promised Land because they are afraid of the people who live there.

Israel's spies have come back with a report saying that the land is just like God said it was, "flowing with milk and honey." The only problem is that giants live there. Ten of Israel's spies suggest a retreat, while only Caleb and Joshua step forward to say that with God all things, even conquering giants, are possible. The people take the advice of the ten over the two and then begin to grumble against God and their leaders, Moses and Aaron. The people even start to plan a trip back to Egypt. At this point, God explodes, and his thundering response proves that he is not just a teddy bear. While God offers his people protection, encouragement and comfort, we cannot own him and treat him as a teddy bear. He does not exist to be a part of our lives. He wants us to be a part of his life.

■ What is the problem with trying to own God?

_____

_____

_____

■ Do you ever treat God like you own him?

❑ yes
❑ no

Explain your answer.

_____

_____

_____

■ How does following God challenge this thought pattern?

_____

_____

_____

Spend a few minutes evaluating how you have talked to God in the past. Do you find that your prayer life consists more of trying to get God into your life instead of seeking to get in on God's life? Spend some time praying that God would help you see and pursue his life and plans.

GOD IS...HUGE

_____

_____

_____

_____

_____

_____

_____

_____

_____

_____

_____

_____

_____

_____

_____

This page is designed to give you space to take notes during your "God is . . ." group session or to journal your reflections on the highlights of this week's study.

GOD IS...

PERSONAL

a God not
disconnected from
our struggle

GOD IS... PERSONAL

God in desparate situations

Last week we looked at how God is huge. We saw how God shatters every box in which we try to place him. As we looked at God in that way, though, you may have had this question: "If God is that huge and all I learned about God is true, then can this same huge God be a personal God?" Sometimes we're not too sure that huge things can be personal. So this week we'll explore how God is personal.

There is no better place to start talking about how God is personal than in desperate situations, because it is in desperate situations that our need for a personal God is most obvious.

Read Matthew 8:23-27

Have you ever been whitewater rafting? If you haven't, you need to go. Whitewater rafting is thrilling and can even be scary at times. The first time I went whitewater rafting was with my church group. We rafted down the Ocoee River.

The morning began with the rafting guides taking our group through the mandatory safety classes. In these classes, the guides talked about what to do if we fell out of the raft or got stuck in a rapid. They talked about the injuries we could sustain and many other things. I think they were trying hard to scare us so we wouldn't goof off on the river. It worked, because I can remember that by the time they finished that discussion I was pretty sure I was going to die that day. Some of the adult leaders who were with us felt the same way. They tried hard not to show their fear, but the tears in the eyes of some of the women gave the truth away.

As if this wasn't bad enough, at the end of the safety class the leaders had us sign a release form that read something like "If you die, we cannot be held responsible." You can imagine that our group was pretty tense when it came time to start.

The guides tried to reassure us by telling us that no one had ever died on any rapid except the first one—a comforting thought with which to begin the journey. While we tried to show our courageous spirits, we were scared to death.

I was in the first raft from our group. We made it down the first rapid successfully. When we got to the bottom of the only "deadly" rapid, some of my anxiety was relieved, so I relaxed and watched some of the other rafts in our group.

My brother was riding in a raft a few groups back. I'll never forget what I saw that day. My brother's raft was somehow pushed down the wrong portion of the rapid, and before anyone knew what was happening, his raft was bent in half, and he was thrown out in front of it. Now he was in the menacing waters of the "deadly" rapid all by himself. As thoughts of drowning raced through his mind, his face showed how desperate his situation was. His eyes were as big as saucers as he cried for help. Finally, after a ride that took seconds but seemed to last forever, their guide pulled him back into the boat at the bottom of the rapid. My brother has not been whitewater rafting since.

This is as close as I have come to being in the kind of storm mentioned in Matthew 8:23–27. I can imagine that the disciples' position was even worse than my brother's. The waves were crashing around them, and they felt as if their boat would sink. They came to Jesus with what has been called the most honest prayer in the entire Bible: "Lord, save us! We're going to drown!" Their situation was desperate, and they wanted to know, "Does God really care?"

■ Have you ever been in a desperate situation physically, emotionally, or spiritually? Explain that situation.

_____

_____

_____

_____

_____

■ Have you ever felt like Jesus was sleeping during your desperate situation? Explain that situation.

_____

_____

_____

■ Rank the following statements by how much they reflect the way you react in desperate situations.

4 ⬚ □ I go to my parents.
2 □ I rely on myself to make it through.
1 □ I look to my best friend for support.
3 □ I trust God.

The end of the story shows Jesus stepping into the disciples' desperation, speaking to the wind and seas and calming the storm. He has some tough words for his disciples, but nevertheless he works and he cares. At the bottom of the question, "Is God personal?" is the deeper question, "Does God care?" This week we are going to be spending some time looking at a personal God. The truth that we will discover is nothing less than life-changing.

prayer exercise:

Take some time to go through some of the desperate situations that you wrote down in today's devotion. Reflect on how you handled those situations and what those situations taught you about God. Was there ever a time where you felt God was not personal? Maybe you feel that way now. Ask God to reveal himself in a personal way to you this week.

GOD IS... PERSONAL

does God really care?

There are a lot of important things going on in the world today. There are wars in different countries. Powerful men and women lead their cities, states and countries. Major corporations employ millions of people and provide services to consumers all over the world.

With so many serious things going on, doesn't it seem like God has a lot of major issues to be concerned with? Can you imagine what it would be like to be him? He has millions of followers all over the world who often come to him in prayer. It is easy to feel very small and forgotten when we consider the grand scope of things.

■ With everything that is going on in the world, do you think God really cares about your life and the little details of it?

   ☒ yes
   ☐ no

Explain your answer.

_____

_____

_____

When I was a little boy, my grandfather was my hero. I used to think he was the strongest man in the world. He used to tell me that he wrestled alligators and chased down lions. The funny thing is that I believed him. Nobody compared to my grandfather. Through my 4-year-old eyes, I figured he was in charge of the whole world. Whenever I needed something, I ran to him. If I was playing outside and got scared, I ran to him looking for protection. When we played games, I asked him what the rules were. My grandmother tells me stories even now about how often I talked to him and asked him question after question. I never once wondered if he had time for me. He made me feel like the most important person in the world. I never hesitated to go to him about anything. He was so personal with me. He was my best friend.

Read Luke 12:22-25

In this passage, Jesus tells his followers not to worry. That's not always an easy command to follow, but Jesus gives us the reason behind the instruction. He tells his followers what God thinks about believers and how he cares for them personally.

■ Why do many Christians wonder if God is interested in them personally and in their daily activities?

_____

_____

_____

_____

■ Do you ever struggle with seeing God as someone who provides and looks after you?

   ☑ yes
   ☐ no

■ How do these verses say God relates to the birds of the air?

_____

_____

_____

_____

_____

■ If God relates to birds that way, how does he relate to his children? List some ways God has shown himself as personal in your life.

_____

_____

_____

prayer exercise:

Spend some time thanking God for how he provides for you personally. Use the space below to list ways in which he has shown you that you are important to him. Try to list some specific ways he has provided for you.

GOD IS... PERSONAL

Mark
10:13-16

no one
is too small

■ Do you believe that God cares about you? Why?

Yes

■ Have you ever experienced a time when you felt as though God did not care about you? Explain that situation.

If you have ever been to Six Flags, Walt Disney World, or any other theme park, then you know that on almost every ride worth riding there is a height requirement. I can remember when, as a little fellow, I just hated those signs. Sure, they looked pleasant, with a picture of Goofy or Daffy Duck holding a measuring stick. But the person supervising the ride wasn't so nice. You were either tall enough to ride, or you were not. And if you were not, then you had just spent two hours waiting in line for nothing. I can remember more than a few times being sent down to wait at the exit for the ride to meet friends who had just had the time of their lives on the ride.

Soon, I grew taller than Goofy's measuring stick, and I got to ride the rides at theme parks. The rides were just as fun as I always imagined they were. That's one reason I'm glad I'll never return to the height I was at age seven. However, even now as I walk past those measuring signs, the thoughts of days gone by bring back feelings of frustration. I just wanted to ride the rides, but I was told I was too small.

While everyone may not have had this particular theme-park experience, all of us probably have felt a twinge of something very similar in our relationships with God. Maybe we've felt too small. Or maybe we felt as though God couldn't possibly want to take the time out of his day to think about our petty concerns. But the truth of the Bible strikes hard against these thoughts.

Read Mark 10:13-16

Fill in the blanks:
Mark 10:13 says, "People were bringing little children to Jesus to have Him _____ them, but the disciples _____ them."

■ Compare and contrast Jesus' response to the children with the disciples' response to them.

_____

_____

_____

■ What does Jesus' response here tell us about God?

_____

_____

_____

■ How does seeing this picture help you as you relate to God?

_____

_____

_____

I love Jesus in this story. The disciples are there with their measuring sticks, trying to determine what kind of person could come to Jesus. Some people come with their children, and the disciples are furious—because they think Jesus certainly doesn't have time for kids. Or does He?

Jesus' reply shatters the disciples' perceptions. In fact, Jesus said if you don't come to him like a child, then you can't come at all. Jesus reverses the norm. The question is not, "Am I too **small** to come to Jesus?" It's, "Am I too **big** to come to Jesus?" God is concerned with the details of our lives. As little children come to their parents with any problem, so God invites us to share the details of our lives with him.

■ What details of your life have you been hesitant to share with God?

_____

_____

_____

■ Have you become too big for God by working to solve all your problems on your own?

☒ yes
☐ no

■ What are some ways you are tempted to become too big for God?

_____

_____

_____

_____

_____

Spend some time opening the details of your life up to God. Remember that nothing is too small. Tell him all about your life: your joys, your struggles, your pains, and your sorrows. God is waiting to meet with you.

God wants us
to stop running

1 Peter
5:1-7

When I was a little boy, I had a friend who had a pet hamster named Sylvester. I loved going to my friend's house and watching Sylvester run on his wheel. He would run and run and run for what seemed like forever. He ran so fast I thought his feet were going to fall off.

It was strange though, because Sylvester never got anywhere. No matter how hard he ran, he always ended up in the same place. Sylvester would run for hours only to end up back where he started. I don't think he ever figured it out. He looked frustrated and tired when he finished running.

Why do we act like Sylvester in our Christian lives? When we get stressed or upset about something, we run on our little wheels and exhaust ourselves with worry and anxiety. We wonder if God is personal enough for us to take our cares and anxieties to him. God is looking for his children to get off of the wheel of worry and anxiety. He is waiting for his people to cast their cares onto him.

■ Has there ever been a time in your life where you chose to take your cares to the wheel of worry and anxiety instead of giving them to God? Explain that situation.

_____

_____

_____

■ What happened when you went to run on the wheel instead of trusting God?

_____

_____

Peter was writing to a group of Christians who were being persecuted for their faith. They were faced with an extremely stressful situation. These believers could have even lost their lives for their faith in Christ. The Roman emperor, Nero, was ruthless. He burned Christians at the stake for their belief in Jesus. Needless to say, these early Christians needed to hear how much God cared for them. That's the truth Peter focuses on in verse 7.

■ How would you have felt if you had been in Rome during this time period and faced death because of what you believed?

_____

_____

_____

_____

■ Would you have questioned God's love for you in that situation? Why?

_____

_____

_____

_____

■ Fill in the blanks:
1 Peter 5:7 says, "Cast all your _____ on him because he _____ for you."

■ Are there some anxieties in your life that you need to cast on God?

❑ yes
❑ no

If your answer is yes, list those anxieties.

_____

_____

_____

■ List some ways you can stop running on the wheel in your life.

_____

_____

_____

prayer exercise:

Express to God how thankful you are that he cares about you. Give him anything that is weighing you down. Ask him to give you the courage to be a person who says yes to his personal invitation of casting your cares to him.

GOD IS... PERSONAL

a God
who is involved

One of the greatest truths of all time is that God is active in the lives of Christians. Think about this for a moment: once upon a time, there was only God. He created the sky, the moon, the waters, the sun, the trees, the animals, and the entire universe. He is the creator of everything. He created man and woman. The good news, however, is that God did not stop his activity with creation. He still acts in the world today. That is such an awesome truth. God is personal and active. The Creator of all things has a personal interest and is active in the lives of his children.

■ List some instances in your life where you could clearly sense that God was involved and working with you in your walk with him.

_____

_____

_____

_____

Read 1 Samuel 3

This passage contains a story many people love to read. It gives us such a wonderful picture of God speaking to young Samuel. Throughout this book, there is the sense that God is in control of the nation of Israel. He has a plan for the nation and uses people like Samuel to proclaim his word. This mighty God shows by his actions that he is personally interested in the lives of his followers.

Can you imagine what it must have been like to actually hear the voice of God as Samuel did? It was a night that would mark this young boy for the rest of his life. God spoke and intervened in an ordinary boy's life.

■ As you read this passage, what part of this story speaks to you most? Why?

_____

_____

_____

■ What are some ways that God speaks now?

_____

_____

_____

■ What does the truth that God speaks to us tell us about his character and how he feels about his followers?

_____

_____

_____

In 1980, Jimmy Carter was the President of the United States. There was a third-grader named Sarah who wanted to meet him more than anything in the world. One day Sarah found out that President Carter was going to be coming through her hometown on a speaking engagement. Sarah begged her mom to take her to see President Carter. Sarah's mom explained to her that there would be too many people there and that the president would be too busy. The mother said that President Carter was the most powerful man in the world and that Sarah would not be able to even get close to him. But Sarah would not give up. She begged and begged, and her mom finally gave in and agreed to take Sarah to the president's speech.

As the big day drew near, Sarah decided she would make the president a sign that said, "I love you, Mr. President." Her mom thought it was a cute idea but that the president would never see it. The day of the president's visit, Sarah and her mom left early to get a good seat. When they got to the auditorium, Sarah and her mom found a good spot that was surprisingly almost empty. They had a great view, and Sarah thought it was the perfect place for the president to see her and her sign. Sarah's mom thought her daughter was so cute as she sat there waiting for the president, but she was upset because she knew that Sarah would be very disappointed when the president never even came near her.

After a long period of waiting with anticipation, the president finally arrived. Everyone was cheering and clapping for the most powerful man in the world. Sarah stood up and held her sign up over her head. To the amazement of the crowd—and especially her mother—President Carter stopped in his tracks when he read the sign. He walked right over to Sarah, gave her a big smile, and said, "Thank you."

Sarah never doubted for a moment that she would meet the president. She was so excited about how everything happened. She went back home and told all of her friends.

■ Is God too big or powerful to be involved in your life, or will he talk to you? How do you know?

_____

_____

_____

prayer exercise:

Praise God for how he is active in your life. Express to him how awesome it is that he is not only Creator but also a God who is involved in people's lives.

GOD IS...PERSONAL

_____

_____

_____

_____

_____

_____

_____

_____

_____

_____

_____

_____

_____

This page is designed to give you space to take notes during your "God is . . ." group session or to journal your reflections on the highlights of this week's study.

GOD IS...

HOLY

a God worth
worshiping

GOD IS...HOLY

when God
shows up

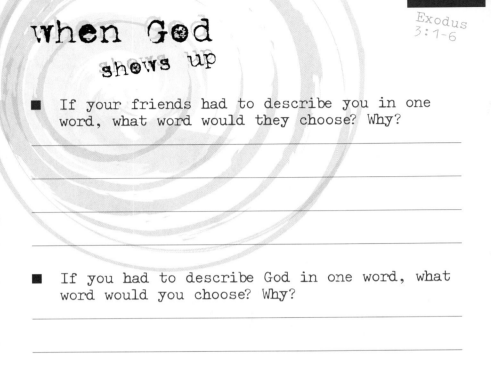

■ If your friends had to describe you in one word, what word would they choose? Why?

_____

_____

_____

_____

■ If you had to describe God in one word, what word would you choose? Why?

_____

_____

_____

_____

It's hard to narrow all we are down into just one word. Any word is a partial description at best, because there are so many facets to our personalities. But sometimes, one word illustrates at least the essence of a person. Think about the following examples:

Michael Jordan: Air
Jim Carrey: Wacky
Mother Teresa: Compassion

This week we are going to take some time to discover what it means when we say that God is holy. When the Bible talks about God, it describes God using this word more than any other. "Holy" is used to describe who God is, where God is, and what God touches. But what is holiness?

■ Take a moment to write a one-sentence
definition of holiness.

_____

_____

_____

We'll get back to that definition at the end of
the week.

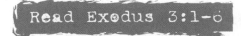

Read Exodus 3:1-6

Have you ever been taken by surprise? Maybe you walked into a dark
room, thinking everyone had forgotten your birthday, unaware that there
in the dark sat all your friends waiting to yell, "Surprise!" and scare you half
to death. Maybe you were taken by surprise when a friend whom you had
not seen for a long time showed up at your door to see how you were doing.
Maybe someone surprised you by sneaking up and yelling in your ear right
at your moment of deepest concentration.

In any case, surprises tell us a lot about ourselves. They show us how we
react when we haven't had time to plan our responses.

In Exodus 3, Moses is surprised by God. While Moses was working as a
shepherd in an isolated corner of the desert, his attention was drawn to a
burning bush. Moses was curious about how the bush was burning without
being consumed, so he went to check out this strange phenomenon. He had
no idea he was about to be surprised by God.

As Moses stood in front of the bush, God called him and told him to take
off his sandals because he was on holy ground. God then told Moses exactly
who it was that was speaking to him. Upon hearing this, "Moses hid his face,
because he was afraid to look at God." Moses knew he had encountered
something that was out of his league. He knew he did not belong. He knew
that if his sandals were not worthy to walk on the ground God occupied,
then he himself was not worthy to look on God.

All of these responses came naturally to Moses. No one told Moses what to
do in this moment. No one prescribed for him how to react to God.
Overwhelmed by God's otherness, God's holiness, Moses bowed in submission.

■ Can you think of some other people who were surprised by God and what their responses were? Explain those situations.

_____

_____

_____

_____

Many times as Christians, we get so at home with God that we forget as we relate to him that we are not on equal footing. This week, as we study God's holiness, we will be reminded that we are not like God. God's holiness reminds us that the difference between us and God is vast and that on our own we will never be able to relate to him.

prayer exercise:

Take some time today to stand in awe of God. This may mean you want to walk to a place where you can look on God's creation. Or you may want to stand outside this evening to look up at the stars and marvel at the vastness of God. Whatever you do, be creative in finding a place where you can be overwhelmed by God, a place where you can realize that you are not God. Spend some time in that place recognizing that you are a creation and he is the Creator.

GOD IS...HOLY

the holy other

Rudy is a movie about the struggles of a boy whose dream is to play football at the University of Notre Dame. These struggles include being rejected for admission three different times. After receiving his third rejection letter, Rudy seeks solace from a Catholic priest who has become his friend and confidante. Rudy asks the priest a series of questions about this rejection and concludes that maybe he just hadn't prayed hard enough. At this point, the priest offers a bit of advice that provides some keen insight. He says, "Son, in 35 years of religious study, I've come up with only two hard, incontrovertible facts. There is a God, and I'm not him."

Knowing we are not God is the beginning of understanding what God's holiness is all about. Yesterday, we took some time to talk about how Moses acted toward God. The thought we came away with is where we begin today. Moses realized God's otherness, and Moses knew that he was not God. But what was the difference between God and Moses? Today we focus on that question.

■ Thinking back to yesterday's lesson, list some ways God and Moses were different.

_____

_____

_____

The truth is that there are a million ways God and Moses were different. God is infinite; Moses was finite. God can see the future; Moses couldn't. God is all powerful; Moses was not. The list goes on and on. However, one striking characteristic that differentiates God from Moses, and God from all human beings, is that God is sinless and we are not. Today we want to focus on this tough reality.

■ How does this story make you feel?

_____

_____

_____

■ What does this story tell you about God?

_____

_____

_____

The story in this passage is frightening. Two of Aaron's sons walk into the presence of God the wrong way and die as a result. We are not exactly sure what these two men did wrong. They may have entered with the wrong censors, or at the wrong time, or they could have been in a place only Aaron could go. Perhaps they were drunk, recklessly disrespecting God's presence. But the truth communicated here is that God's holiness cannot reside with our unholiness (our sin and disobedience).

Throughout the book of Exodus and the first part of Leviticus, God prescribed measures for his people to come into his presence. These two men did not take those measures seriously, and it cost them their lives. They disobeyed, and God cannot have sin in his presence.

The passage ends with Moses telling Aaron that he must distinguish between the holy and the common, the clean and the unclean. What Moses is saying here is that the Israelites must understand they are not God and that, in approaching God, they must come to him on his terms. Israel must come to the realization that God's purity cannot reside with its impurity. Coming into the presence of God is a huge deal and must be respected as such. In short, God and sin cannot reside together. That leaves us with a major problem.

The second part of learning about holiness is understanding its implications about purity. God is not only different than us, he is also totally pure. There is no sin in God. God is pure righteousness. Everything he does is right. There is no fault in God.

■ What does understanding God's purity teach you about how you relate to God?

_____

_____

_____

prayer exercise:

Spend some time today getting in touch with how sinful and impure you really are. As an exercise in humility, find a place where no one will see you and get on your face before God. Ask God to reveal two things to you: your own sinfulness and his holiness.

GOD IS... HOLY

what only
Christ can do

Have you ever been in a place where you felt you didn't belong? For some of us, a couple of places immediately spring to mind: the honor roll, the football team, on a date.

Not too long ago my wife and I went out to dinner with two friends. We had bought a coupon book that allowed us to eat at a lot of restaurants for half-price. I know this is something you normally see older people do, but times were tight, and we were trying to do whatever we could to save some money.

At the front of the coupon book were discounts at some restaurants we normally would not go to on our own, nice restaurants in prime downtown locations. On this night, because we had a coupon, we decided to go to one of these restaurants.

As soon as we walked into the restaurant, I sensed that we were out of our league. The hostess asked us if we had a reservation, which of course we didn't. She seated us in the center of the restaurant, where we were surrounded by people who looked like they belonged there.

Our waitress took our drink orders. (You know you're out of your league when the place has four different types of water to choose from.) Everything on the menu was *a la carte,* meaning you paid for everything— the entree, the salad, the potato—separately. So between the four of us, we ordered two entrees (one of which was free), two salads and two potatoes and still ended up spending more than we would have at Outback Steakhouse. We were pretty sure the waitresses pegged us as coupon-book people the moment we walked in.

■ Have you ever felt as though you didn't belong with God? Which of the following statements best describes your relationship with God?

    ❑ I never feel that I don't belong with God.
    ❑ I sometimes feel that I don't belong with God.
    ❑ I always feel that I don't belong with God.

- Do you think the answer you picked is how you are supposed to feel with God? Explain your answer.

_____

_____

_____

- What does Jesus have to say about the answers to those questions?

_____

_____

_____

Read Hebrews 10:19-25

The book of Hebrews is awesome. Although it is pretty heavy stuff, its implications for Christian living are staggering. Yesterday we talked about how approaching God was a holy matter and how God and sin could not exist together. We read the story about how Aaron's two sons died because they didn't take the matter of approaching God seriously. Throughout the Old Testament, specific guidelines clarified how people were to come before God. The elements of priest, sacrifice, and temple made approaching God possible.

In the Old Testament, the glory of God descended upon the temple. The temple was where the magnified presence of God dwelled. To approach God, people would bring an offering to the priest. The priest, who himself had to be cleansed, went to God on behalf of each family. Once a year, the high priest went into the Most Holy Place, or Holy of Holies, to make a sacrifice for all the people. With all of these methods, access to God was restricted.

Jesus changed things. Hebrews tells how Jesus acted as the great high priest on our behalf, trumping the old way of doing things. Before Jesus, priests made the offering for the people. But as our high priest, Jesus became our offering. Before Jesus, people came to God with offerings. But in Jesus, God came to us with an offering. Before Jesus, the priest was a sinner. But Jesus our high priest is perfect. Before Jesus, priests would die. Jesus our High Priest lives forever.

Before Jesus, access to God was restricted because people had to go to the temple and make sacrifices through a priest. Hebrews tells us that, because of Jesus, we can boldly come into the presence of God.

The truth Hebrews brings out is that Jesus does what nothing else could do. Jesus makes a relationship between Holy God and ordinary, unholy people possible. Jesus does this by transferring his holiness onto us. Now we can come boldly into the presence of Holy God because we are marked by his Holy Son.

The essence of today's devotion is this: Jesus makes us belong with God. When we become Christians, we are no longer enslaved by our own sinfulness. We need to keep in mind that without Jesus we are wretched, but with Jesus we go from being defined by our sin to being defined by Christ. We are Christians, and that is the greatest news in the whole world.

■ Take some time to list the concepts we talked about above. Fill in the chart below by referring to today's lesson.

	Before Jesus	With Jesus
sacrifice		
priest		
temple		

prayer exercise:

Go through each of these three areas and thank Jesus for his work, recognizing the access to God that we have because of him.

GOD IS...HOLY

a tough command

Who do you want to be like? Do you want to play basketball like Michael Jordan? Do you want to play soccer like Pelé? Do you want to be an actress like Julia Roberts? Do you want to sing like Michelle Branch? We all have role models. We admire some attributes in a person, so we seek to be like them to a certain extent.

That's why we spend hours working to develop a crossover dribble like Allen Iverson or perfecting a bicycle kick to emulate the one we saw Marcelo Balboa do for the United States in the 1994 World Cup. It's why, when we hear Britney Spears sing, we go home and practice singing in the hopes that, if we get the right breaks, we too can make it as big as she did. Wanting to be like someone can affect the way we order our lives.

■ List three people whom you look to as role models. Beside each name, explain why you see them that way.

1. _____

2. _____

3. _____

Read Leviticus 11:44

Fill in the blanks:
Leviticus 11:44 says, "Be _____, because I am _____."

■ Who does this verse say our spiritual role model should be?

_____

_____

■ How does this command make you feel?

_____

_____

_____

   As Christians, we live our lives for God. But even with that commitment,
Leviticus 11:44 is a tough command: "Be holy, because I am holy." This
statement wouldn't be so bad if Moses, David, Esther or some other Bible
hero made it. We might even be able to carry a command like that out to
some degree. But the fact that this command comes from God puts us in a
tough position.

   This verse means that, just as we imitate our role models in athletics or
music, we must model our lives of holiness after God. This is a high calling
and a pretty scary task, especially as we look at our souls and remember
that we are not at all like God.

Read Jeremiah 18:1-12 and Romans 12:1-2

■ Compare and contrast the picture of the
   people of Israel in Jeremiah 18:1-12 with
   Paul's command in Romans 12:1-2.

_____

_____

_____

■ How do these comparisons help us define what
   holiness means to us as believers?

_____

_____

_____

Jeremiah 18:1–12 gives us a picture of what unholy living looks like. It is resistant to the creative hands of the Father. Romans 12:1–2 shows us what a holy life looks like: moldable clay in the hands of the potter. Paul tells us that, in response to the mercy of God in our lives, we are to be living sacrifices that are holy to God. This means that we lay our lives on the altar to God and allow him to make us more and more into what he wants us to be.

This process of allowing God to take over more and more of our lives is called **transformation.** No matter how long you have been a Christian, this transformation is still taking place. It is not easy, but as we grow in Christ, we learn to let him invade our lives more and more fully.

Even now, there are places in our lives that are in rebellion to God. The message of holiness is that God wants to transform those places too. The message of salvation tells us the battle for our lives has been won, but the message of transformation reminds us that we must still pull out the rebel troops and replace them with the presence of God.

prayer exercise:

Take some time to consider this question: What areas in your life would you still consider to be in rebellion to God? List those areas:

_____

_____

_____

Would you lay those areas on the altar to God today? Would you live your life today as a sacrifice, letting God take over more and more of who you are? Use this prayer to help you end this devotion:

Lord, You are a Holy God. I want to be holy, because You are holy. My soul longs to be transformed by you. I know this process will take as long as I am living. I know some days will be better than others. I know that different areas of my life will be in rebellion to You at different times. But today I commit myself to live as a sacrifice offered to you because of the incredible mercy you have shown me. Lord, this is the attitude that I want to be the characteristic of my life. I need You to change me. Thank you, God, for the work you have already done in me. I love you.

GOD IS... HOLY

when we stumble

All of us have our clumsy moments. How many of us have almost fallen down after stepping on a rise in the pavement as we walked along paying attention to everything but where we were walking? Or how many times have we stepped off a curb suddenly without realizing it, wrenching our backs in the process?

We have a couple different reactions when we stumble. Some try to play it off by taking off into a little jog for a few steps, acting as though the change of pace was planned. Others can't recover as quickly and wind up on their faces. Some blame the cement. Others just laugh it off.

We've been walking for years, so it's not that we don't know how to walk. But every once in a while, we get caught up in things that take our attention from away from walking. Most of the time we can handle it, but sometimes we stumble.

The same is true in our Christian walk. Sometimes we stumble, and sometimes we fall. The Bible tells of the stumbles and failures of almost every major character who enters the narrative.

Have you ever wondered why that is the case? Why does the Bible tell us about Moses murdering an Egyptian, Abraham trying to pass his wife off as his sister, David sleeping with Bathsheba, and Peter denying Jesus?

I think it's because the Bible is not about these characters as much as it is about their God. Moses, Abraham, David, Peter, and the rest are just supporting actors. The main character of the Bible is God. The Bible tells us who God is many times by showing how he acts right in the middle of the lives of ordinary people. So if we didn't know Moses and Abraham stumbled, we might not know that God can use us even when we stumble.

How are we to respond when we stumble in our relationship with a Holy God? Today, we are going to spend some time looking at the prayer of a stumbler named David.

- After reading Psalm 51, which statement do you think was true of David?

  - ☐ David never stumbled in his walk with God.
  - ☐ David didn't care if he stumbled in his relationship with God.
  - ☐ David was broken over his sin against Holy God and cried out for forgiveness.

- In verse 10, what kind of heart did David ask God to create within Him?

_____

_____

_____

Psalm 51 was written by David after Nathan the prophet confronted him about his adultery with Bathsheba and the murder of her husband. This is the same David who was called a man after God's own heart, yet here he suffers one of the most devastating spiritual setbacks recorded in the Bible. This psalm shows the agony of David's heart, a pain that plagues all of us after we stumble.

Did you notice his prayer? What did David do? He confessed his sin and threw himself on the mercy of God with a broken spirit and a contrite heart. Then he asked God to change his heart, which is something only God could do. David's response teaches us what we should do when we stumble. We must admit our sin, turn from it, confess it to God and throw ourselves at his merciful feet, begging him to change our hearts. A broken spirit and a contrite heart come from knowing that our sin is not just sin against ourselves or some other person but sin against God himself.

When we sin, we sin against the One who gave us life. God has called us to be holy, and we have acted in defiance. We have done what he hates. But he is a merciful God, full of goodness and grace, and as we confess our sins to him, he credits us with righteousness.

■ How can you implement what you have learned from this psalm in your life the next time you stumble?

_____

_____

_____

■ Who is the major character of your life? Is your life a story about the power of God, or are you still living for yourself? Take some time to write out your own personal testimony of holiness. Talk about your stumbles, Jesus' action in your life and your continual pursuit of transformation.

_____

_____

_____

■ Look back at the definition of holiness you wrote out at the beginning of the week. Is there anything that you need to change about that definition now that we have spent a week studying God's holiness? Write out a revised definition. Use a dictionary if you need to.

_____

_____

_____

_____

Spend some time thinking about what we've learned this week. Walk through each of the themes that we've been introduced to over the last five days: God as other, God as pure, how Jesus makes a relationship with God possible, how we are called to be holy ourselves and how we relate to God when we stumble. Pray through each thought as God leads you.

GOD IS...HOLY

_____

_____

_____

_____

_____

_____

_____

_____

_____

_____

_____

_____

_____

This page is designed to give you space to take notes during your "God is . . ." group session or to journal your reflections on the highlights of this week's study.

GOD IS...

GRACIOUS

a God with a
big heart

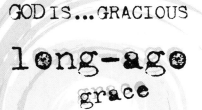

GOD IS...GRACIOUS

long-ago
grace

Last week, we focused on the holiness of God. This week we will look at God's grace. Take some time to answer the following questions as we start our discussion.

■ Write down your definition of grace.

_____

_____

_____

■ Do you think that God's grace is more of an Old Testament theme or a New Testament theme? Why?

_____

_____

_____

■ What is the first biblical example of God's grace? What are the details of that story?

_____

_____

_____

My grandmother is a special person in my life. When I was growing up, my favorite thing to do was to take the two-hour trip to her house to visit her. I loved playing in her yard. I would act like I was a policeman, and I always seemed to catch the "bad guys." My grandmother was awesome because she always let me go outside and play. She had only one rule: Stay in the yard. It wasn't a bad rule, because she had a huge yard. And I knew the rule. There was no question about it.

One morning, I ran out of the house to play, and I heard what I always heard when I ran out: "Stay in the yard." But for some reason, that day I decided to venture outside of the yard. I knew it was wrong, and I knew I would get into trouble. But I didn't care.

Later that day, as I looked up from the fort that I was building, I saw my grandmother walking toward me. I knew I was in big trouble. She leaned down, got on my eye level and said, "I am really disappointed in you." I started crying because I knew I had let her down.

But then she said something to me that gave me my first picture of grace. She asked, "Would you like to go fishing?" I expected punishment, but she gave me something I did not deserve—grace. My grandmother was not rewarding me for my bad behavior. She was loving me despite my actions and showing me grace in the process.

Read Genesis 3:1-21

■ Do you think it's odd that one of the first pictures of God's grace is found this early in the Bible? Why or why not?

_____

_____

_____

■ How does God display his grace in verse 21?

_____

_____

_____

_____

Usually, when we think of the grace of God, our minds turn toward the New Testament. The New Testament is filled with words about his grace and love. But there is one truth we must not overlook: God has **always** been gracious. Here, his grace is evident at the beginning of the Bible in the story of creation. Adam and Eve are in the garden. They know what they are not supposed to do, but they do it anyway. But despite their sin and disobedience, God extends his grace toward them. He makes clothes for them to wear.

This truth is amazing. Yes, God's awesome display of grace through his son at Calvary is unbelievable. But that's not the only time he showed grace. We can't forget that God has always been gracious. The grace we experience is not just a New Testament grace. It is a grace that originated long, long ago.

■ Has there been a time in your life where you were overwhelmed by the grace of God? Explain that situation.

_____

_____

_____

prayer exercise:

Take some time to express your thankfulness for the magnitude of God's grace. Express to him what his grace means to you.

GOD IS...GRACIOUS

Luke
15:11-32

2 stories
of mercy and grace

Yesterday, we discovered that grace is getting something that you don't deserve. Today, we are talking about mercy.

■ Write down your definition of mercy.

_____

_____

_____

I love my dad. We have a great relationship. I am so thankful for the kind of father he has proven to be over the years. My worst feelings as a son usually came after I disappointed or disobeyed him.

One time when I was ten years old, I made a huge mistake—I willingly disobeyed my father. A friend of mine lived two miles from my house, and I would usually take a dirt road to go and see him. My dad did not mind me taking this back road as long as I obeyed one little rule: Don't go to your friend's house or return home if you have to ride your bike in the dark. The rule was simple and easy to understand. I could not, under any circumstances, ride my bike in the dark.

Once, when I knew my dad was out of town, I rode my bike home from my friend's house in the dark. I figuredthat I could tell my mom I was at my next-door neighbor's house and she would never know otherwise. On this dark night, I took my time on the way home, thankful that my dad was out of town. But when I got home, I saw something that almost made me fall off of my bike—my dad's car was in the driveway.

As I walked inside, my dad stood there waiting, asking me where I had been. I was scared to death and didn't know what to do. I had made a huge mistake, and I was really upset at myself. He told me to go to my room.

I sat on my bed forever waiting for him to come and give me a spanking. He came back to my room, sat down next to me and told me how disappointed in me he was as I bawled my eyes out. I had disobeyed my father, whom I loved very much.

But an amazing thing happened. He did not give me a spanking. I begged him to forgive me, and he did. I hugged him so hard when he said those beautiful words, "I forgive you." Not only did he not give me a spanking; he took me to get some ice cream. I will never forget that display of grace and mercy.

■ Which is the example of mercy in this story?

❑ Not getting a spanking.

❑ Going for ice cream.

■ Which is the example of grace in this story?

❑ Not getting a spanking.

❑ Going for ice cream.

Read Luke 15:11-32

■ What is the example of mercy in this passage?

_____

_____

_____

■ What is the example of grace in this passage?

_____

_____

_____

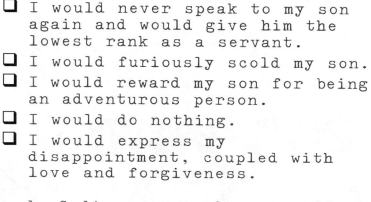

■ If you were the father in this story, how would you have reacted?

❑ I would never speak to my son again and would give him the lowest rank as a servant.

❑ I would furiously scold my son.

❑ I would reward my son for being an adventurous person.

❑ I would do nothing.

❑ I would express my disappointment, coupled with love and forgiveness.

■ How do God's grace and mercy affect your everyday Christian life?

_____

_____

_____

_____

The story of the prodigal son is one of the most famous stories in the entire Bible. It is a story of amazing love, forgiveness, mercy and grace. Some have suggested that it should be called not the story of the prodigal son but of the "Waiting Father." The picture of God we see as this father runs to meet his son is one that is hard to comprehend. How can God love us this much?

If we take the time to read this story slowly and carefully, we will find that this image of God is one that can truly form us as Christians. We follow and serve a God who is full of grace and mercy. In both of these stories, we see grace and mercy exhibited to the fullest. In the first story, the mercy was not getting a spanking, and the grace was the ice-cream cone my dad got for me. In the story of the prodigal son, the father showed mercy by deciding not to punish the son and grace by holding a feast in his honor. This passage teaches us that God is a God of both grace and mercy.

■ Write about a time in your life where God extended both his grace and mercy to you.

_____

_____

_____

prayer exercise:

Praise God for his amazing grace and mercy. Think back on some times in your life where God has extended his mercy and grace to you. Thank him for his love.

the mighty
power of grace

In last week's devotions, we discussed how, in the Old Testament, God was characterized as not being very approachable. A person could come into his presence only when bringing gift offerings or animals to sacrifice. People were constantly making sacrifices for the forgiveness of their sins. These sacrifices had to be made under the administration of priests. It was very different than the way we come to God now.

■ Why don't we make sacrifices when we go to church now? You may want to refer to last week's devotions for help with this answer.

_____

_____

_____

■ Why is God approachable now?

_____

_____

_____

Read Hebrews 4:14-16

Hebrews is a loaded letter. The writer of Hebrews is writing to Jewish believers and telling them to stop acting like other Hebrews, who were continuing to worship God underneath the old law. Worship was different before the death of Christ on the cross. But when Christ came to earth, he was God among us, giving us access to God that had never been possible before. Now, we can approach God with confidence because of Christ.

I love basketball. I really love it when March Madness rolls around and sixty-four teams are placed in a tournament bracket to see who will be the national champion. Recently, some tournament games took place near my hometown. My friend and I decided to go to watch Duke play Notre Dame.

There was just one problem with our plan: We didn't have tickets. We went to the arena anyway in hopes that we could find two tickets. Sure enough, we were able to buy two tickets at face value from someone outside the arena.

But there was another problem. The tickets we bought were on opposite sides of the arena and all the way at the top. I told my friend that we should go to our seats, but that 20 minutes later, we should meet at a particular gate so that I could try to talk a security guard into letting us move down into some unoccupied seats much closer to the court. Now what you have to realize is that, since the terrorist attacks on September 11, 2001, security has really been beefed up. But I decided that trying wasn't going to hurt anything, so we gave it a shot.

I found a security guard and immediately struck up a conversation. I was trying to make a good impression, but it wasn't working. "Those aren't your seats," the security guard said.

"I realize that, but I am asking you to do us a huge favor and grant us access to those two seats that are right beside the floor," I said, throwing in the word "please" as often as I could.

I was shocked when the guard smiled and let us in. We walked right down to just a few rows behind the Duke bench and enjoyed the rest of the game from there. We could not believe our fortune.

■ How does the story above illustrate the access to God that Jesus gives us?

_____

_____

_____

Fill in the blanks:

Hebrews 4:15 says, "For we do not have a high priest who is _____ to sympathize with our weaknesses, but we have one who has been _____ in every way just as we are—yet was without _____."

- What does the truth of that access tell us about God's "Amazing Grace"?

_____

_____

_____

We don't have to be timid when we approach God. We can go to the throne of God with confidence. The blood that Jesus shed gives the children of God access to him anytime, anywhere. We have "courtside seats."

This is an amazing picture of his grace. God is approachable now through the person of Jesus.

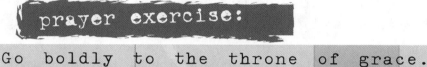

prayer exercise:

Go boldly to the throne of grace. Praise God for giving us forgiveness and access through the blood of his son Jesus.

GOD IS...GRACIOUS

the depth
of grace

prayer exercise:

Start today's devotion with a time
of prayer. Ask the Father to show you
the depth of his grace today.
Express to him how thankful you are
for the unconditional love and grace
he has extended to you.

When I was a little boy, I loved to go swimming. I lived for summer days when I could spend nine hours at the community pool. All my friends hung out there. Our favorite thing to do was to spend time in the deep end. We used to make fun of the kids who were scared of the deep end. And then there was a high dive from which only a brave few would leap. I, of course, was one of those brave few.

We always played a game called "Catch the Penny." We took a penny and placed it in the bottom of the deep end. We took turns leaping off the high dive, swimming all the way to the bottom of the deep end and picking up the penny. Whoever returned to the top quickest was the winner. I loved that game. I remember how my ears popped as I got close to the bottom, a whopping 15 feet below the surface. I felt like Jacques Cousteau at the bottom of the ocean as I plummeted the depths of the pool. I loved the deep end.

■ Do you believe that the grace of Christ
reaches deeply? What leads you to that
conclusion?

_____

_____

■ Give an example of how the grace of Christ reached a deep place in your life or perhaps someone else's. Explain that situation.

_____

_____

_____

Read Luke 7:36-50

This text shows a beautiful picture of the depth of God's grace. The main characters are a sinful woman, a Pharisee named Simon, and Jesus. The first example of Jesus Christ's grace is the fact that he accepted an invitation to go eat at a Pharisee's house. It was an act of grace that Simon never even realized. Simon saw himself as very religious and without sin. Jesus knew that wasn't the truth about Simon, but he went to eat at Simon's house anyway.

Later that evening, a woman who was a known sinner came into the house to find Jesus. To realize the depth of Jesus' grace here, we must understand who this woman was. As soon as she walked into the house, everyone probably started talking. "Look over there, there she is." ... "I can't believe she would dare to come through those doors." ... "How pathetic." ... "What a sinner." She was a known sinner, an outcast from proper society.

However, Jesus suddenly told Simon and everyone else in that room that this sinful woman was forgiven. This had to be a shock. It must have dumbfounded everyone in the room. But that's the way God's grace works. It dumbfounds us. Serial killers can be forgiven. Thieves can be forgiven. I can be forgiven, and you can too. Grace goes even into the depths of our sin.

■ Do you tend to relate more to the sinful woman or Simon the Pharisee? Why?

_____

_____

_____

- What is your answer to Simon's question, "Who is this who even forgives sins?" What gives Jesus the right to forgive people of their sins?

_____

_____

_____

prayer exercise:

Spend some time talking to Jesus about how you feel about him. You might want to thank him for what he has done with your life. You might want to ask him to draw you into a closer walk with him. Worship and praise Jesus for what he did for you on the cross and for what he is doing in your life even now.

GOD IS...GRACIOUS

how gracious
are you?

We love to think of grace as an attribute of God. But when it comes to thinking about grace as an attribute of ours, we get uncomfortable. We love to sing "Amazing Grace" and dwell on the fact that, in his grace, a Holy God has shown us his love. It is much tougher for us to think about what it means for us to follow in his grace.

Julie was the kind of girl who always seemed to find trouble. It's not that she went out looking for it, but it always seemed to find her. While Julie was hanging out with her friends one night, some of them dared her to paint some pretty mean stuff about one of their teachers on a bridge near their hometown. But what started as a silly teenager's practical joke almost landed Julie in jail.

Right as Julie finished painting the nasty words that would line the bridge the next day, a police officer caught her red-handed—literally. Rumors spread around the small town about Julie's arrest, and the words that glared from the top of the bridge left a lasting impact on her school community. Mrs. Bangle, the target of the cruel words on the bridge, was especially hurt by Julie's actions. In fact, Mrs. Bangle missed four days of work because of the hurt Julie had inflicted.

Time passed slowly, but the day of Julie's trial finally came. The whole town waited with baited breath, because they knew Mrs. Bangle would be called to testify against Julie. But nothing could have prepared the town for what happened when Mrs. Bangle took the stand.

Everyone was expecting Mrs. Bangle to lash out in anger, asking the judge to give Julie the most severe sentence possible. But to everyone's astonishment, Mrs. Bangle told the court that she had forgiven Julie, and then she asked the court to do the same. The judge was so shocked by Mrs. Bangle's testimony that he called for a recess so he could ponder the day's events. Julie ended up being sentenced to a few hours of community service, which was nothing compared to the penalty she could have received.

A few days later, once Julie had returned to school, one of her friends passed a note to a third friend saying something bad about Julie. Julie somehow saw the note, and she got angry. When the bell rang, Julie set out on a mission to find the girl who had written mean things about her. Before she knew what was happening, Julie had the author by the throat. She began hitting her in front of the crowd that always gathers to watch fights in high-school hallways. Julie could not believe what her friend had done, and she was determined to make her pay.

 Has someone else ever extended grace to you? Explain that situation.

_____

_____

_____

 Can you relate to the story above? Do you find it hard to extend grace to others? Explain your answer.

_____

_____

_____

 Why do you think it is hard for people to extend grace to others?

_____

_____

_____

Read Matthew 18:21-35

This parable really hits home. We love to receive grace, but many times we are reluctant to be gracious to others. This parable of Jesus is a shocking reminder of how reluctant we are to be gracious to others.

God does so much for us. He forgives us of our sins when we accept Jesus Christ. He continues to forgive us on a daily basis. He provides for us. He teaches us. He watches over us. Yet, we still fail to show the grace we have been given to others.

Slowly re-read this parable a few times. Give it time to impact you. Notice how powerful the message is.

■ Is there anyone in your life that you need to extend grace to? Why? What do you need to do?

_____

_____

_____

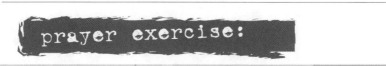

prayer exercise:

Praise God for the grace he has shown you. Ask for his help as you mature into a person who constantly shows grace to others. Pray that God would mold you into a person full of grace and mercy.

This page is designed to give you space to take notes during your "God is . . ." group session or to journal your reflections on the highlights of this week's study.

GOD IS...

JEALOUS

a God who
desires us

GOD IS... JEALOUS

an odd
couple

Couples come in all shapes and sizes. Whenever I sit in an airport, I am amazed at the different kinds of people who are attracted to each other.

Some couples look like they belong together, while others do not. Some couples look like Ken and Barbie, while others are poster children for the motto, "Opposites Attract." Some couples have the perfect clothes; whereas, for some couples, neither is dressed very well. Some couples have the perfect walk, while others look silly while strutting their stuff. Some have the perfect kids, while the kids of other couples are running around everywhere like savages.

Not all couples are graced with the appearance of perfection. Have you ever seen an odd couple? The kind of couple that I'm talking about is blessed with one extreme and its exact opposite. There are thousands of combinations that seem odd together. One combo might be a well-dressed woman whose husband looks like he's stuck in the 1970s. It might be a couple where one person towers over the other. It might be a couple where one is loud and the other hardly ever speaks.

Most of the time when we see couples that strike us as odd, one question runs through our minds: "How did he end up with her?" or vice versa. If we're not in a relationship, we might even ask, "What does he/she have that I don't?" The truth at the bottom of our question is that we're disturbed because, for one reason or another, the couple strikes us as if it doesn't belong together.

Many times the Bible uses the imagery of a husband/wife relationship to describe our relationship with God. It takes no deep insight to realize that God and people make an odd couple.

What could Almighty God see in struggling humanity that would make him want to come alongside us as he does? Why does he take our hand and treat us as his bride? He is so strong, while we are so weak. He is so faithful, while we are so unfaithful. He towers over us as we struggle to stay at his side.

The truth is, I'm not sure what God sees in us that makes him so concerned with us. Yet the Bible proclaims over and over again with unrelenting clarity God's passionate love for his people.

■ Take some time to reflect on some of the boy/girl relationships that you have had in the past. What did you expect from those relationships?

_____

_____

_____

■ How did you expect your boyfriend/girlfriend to act in that relationship?

_____

_____

_____

■ Now take some time to think about your relationship with God. List three things you think God expects from his relationship with you.

1. _____

2. _____

3. _____

Read Exodus 20:1-11

■ What does this passage tell us about what God expects from us?

_____

_____

_____

■ Read through the Ten Commandments listed below and check the ones you struggle with most.

❑ "You shall have no other gods before me."
❑ "You shall not make for yourself an idol."
❑ "You shall not misuse the name of the Lord your God."
❑ "Remember the Sabbath day by keeping it holy."
❑ "Honor your father and your mother."
❑ "You shall not murder."
❑ "You shall not commit adultery."
❑ "You shall not steal."
❑ "You shall not give false testimony against your neighbor."
❑ "You shall not covet."

Exodus 20 gives us a good look at what God expects from a relationship with his people. Previously in the book of Exodus, God delivered his people from Egypt and set up Moses as the leader of his people. Now, the nation of Israel is headed toward the Promised Land, and the people are wondering how to relate to this personal God who has taken up their cause.

As you might have noticed, the beginning of Exodus 20 is what we refer to as the Ten Commandments. The first four commandments relate to our relationship with God, while the last six commandments relate to our relationships with other people. God speaks very clearly through these commandments about what he wants from his people.

In verses 5–6, we see the core value that lies behind the first four commandments. God wants our worship. In fact, he demands our worship. God is saying that he doesn't want us to turn our hearts to anyone or anything other than him. After all, he is a *jealous* God.

This week we are going to spend some time looking at how God is jealous. While many times we would probably not equate the character of God with this trait, throughout the Bible, the word jealous is used to describe God in his relationship toward us. Today, we began our journey by seeing what God expects in our relationship to him. We will develop this thought further throughout the remainder of the week.

Spend a few moments contemplating how God is jealous. Have you ever used the word jealous to describe God in the past? How do you think God is jealous in his relationship with you? Ask God to enlighten you this week about his jealousy and what it means in your relationship with him.

GOD IS...JEALOUS

when love hurts

Love is a many splendored thing, or at least so the saying goes. Actually, love is not always that splendid—especially when someone cheats on you. (Not that I'm bitter or anything.)

Imagine that you are in a romantic relationship with a person whom you have liked for a long time. Everything is going well. You wake up loving life and go to bed dreaming about your life, and every moment in between is filled with thoughts of this other person.

Imagine beginning a relationship that lasts two weeks, then three months and then six months. You become almost consumed with the other person: phone calls at night, notes during the day and expensive presents you really can't afford on birthdays and anniversaries and at Christmas. If you haven't been there, there's nothing like falling in love for the first time.

Now imagine that, on the day before your one-year anniversary, you get some news from your best friends that the girl or guy with whom you have fallen in love has been cheating on you all along. At first you don't believe it, but as time goes on you begin to realize the truth. You've been played. You were in love, but your boyfriend or girlfriend wasn't.

The story above is a combination of the many heartbreaks my friends and I have had over the years. It is also a story that you will probably experience in some form or another at some point in your life. But most surprisingly, it is a story of God and his people.

Read Ezekiel 16

■ What strikes you most in this story about the relationship between God and Israel?

_____

_____

_____

- Have you ever acted like Israel in your relationship with God?

  ☐ yes
  ☐ no

- List three things you have learned about God from this passage of scripture.

1. _____

2. _____

3. _____

The story of Ezekiel 16 is graphic. It would probably be rated R if you saw it at the movies. Yet it is the story of real life. God displayed his love to Israel when she was broken and despised. He made beauty from ashes. But Israel prostituted herself by seeking other gods and giving her love to another. God does not take kindly to Israel's action. Like a jealous lover, he pursues Israel in holy anger.

- Take a moment to think about the following question: What is the opposite of love?

_____

_____

_____

_____

_____

Most people respond that the opposite of love is hate. I wonder if this is true. Hate and love are closely connected. Hate springs from love, for to hate something or to be angry about something often means you first loved that thing.

The story we began with today serves as an example of this truth. If you have ever been cheated on, then you know how close love and hate really are. When the person you love carelessly rips your heart out of your chest and casually tosses it on the floor to be trampled on, you can't help but respond with anger that your love for that other person wasn't returned.

If hate isn't the opposite of love, perhaps the opposite of love is apathy, or not caring at all. Love and hate are both strong emotions. Apathy is the lack of such emotion.

Throughout the Bible, we see God acting with strong emotions. We don't see God acting with apathy. The truth that God is jealous shows us the strong emotions of God. God's jealousy is not the vengeful emotion we are scared it is. Rather, it is love directed at a person not returning that love. It is love that wants to be loved in return. God's jealousy springs from his love.

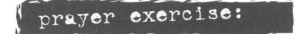

prayer exercise:

Take some time to evaluate your life to see if you have cheated on God. Is God your life priority, or are you consumed with other things? Spend a few minutes in confession and repentance as God reveals the hurt of his heart to you.

GOD IS...JEALOUS

the question
of desertion

There are few worse feelings in the world than feeling as though the one whom you love most has left you. Whether it's a breakup with a boyfriend or girlfriend, your parents' divorce or the rejection of friend, it's hard to get over someone leaving you after you opened your heart to him or her. It might be that, now as you read these words, you are suffering the silent pain of desertion.

More than being angry, your heart longs to know why someone would leave you like this. Questions race through your mind like, *Is there something wrong with me?...Did I do something wrong?...Am I not good enough for* _____?

Answers seem few and far between. The reality of desertion bears down on you, and you wonder why it has to be this way. Where did things go wrong?

Take some time to think about a time when you felt deserted. Answer the following questions as honestly as you can.

■ Describe the time when you most deeply felt as though someone you loved had deserted you.

_____

_____

_____

_____

■ What emotions or feelings did you experience during that time? Check all of the following that apply.

❑ anger
❑ fear
❑ jealousy
❑ confusion
❑ anxiety
❑ panic

■ What questions went through your mind?

_____

_____

_____

■ At what conclusions did you arrive?

_____

_____

_____

By now, you are probably beginning to feel some of the emotions that you checked fester inside of you again. Today's devotion is not meant to bring up old pain, but it is important to get in touch with the feeling of desertion. Thank you for being willing to open up.

■ Do you think God ever feels deserted by us? Why or why not?

_____

_____

_____

Read Jeremiah 2:1-19

■ What questions do you see God asking of himself in this passage as the reality of his people leaving him sets in?

_____

_____

_____

- What conclusion does God come to about his people in verse 13?

_____

_____

_____

The Bible is not shy when it comes to talking about the emotions, feelings and passions of God. In Jeremiah 2, we see God weeping and angry with his people. He wonders, "What fault did they find in me?"

God comes to the conclusion that his people have done two things. First, they have left him, the fountain of living water. Second, they have dug cisterns for themselves. In other words, God's people have slowly abandoned their true love for a lesser love, love of themselves. God's people are convinced that they don't need him, and even in the midst of all their misery, they haven't awakened to the reality that the deepest need of their hearts is for God.

I wonder if we're like God's people in Jeremiah 2. More than just cheating, I wonder if we have wandered away to let our hearts be wooed by a lesser love? I think the old hymn writer got it right when he wrote, "Prone to wander, Lord I feel it, prone to leave the God I love." We too are a people who wander if we are not careful. Jeremiah 2 tells us how our jealous God feels when he is deserted for another.

prayer exercise:

Go back to the questions that you found God asking of his people. Take some time to let God ask those questions of you. Spend some time evaluating whether you have slowly drifted away from God. Pray that God would keep his passion fresh on your heart each day.

GOD IS... JEALOUS

the possibility
of restoration

The most anticipated moment in sports in 2002 may have been Michael Jordan's return to the United Center in Chicago. Jordan's new team, the Washington Wizards, was scheduled to play the Chicago Bulls. Chicago is where Jordan spent his whole career until he ventured to make the comeback of a lifetime with Washington. In Chicago, Michael is an icon. They even have a statue of him in front of the arena.

But how would the Chicago crowd react to the sight of Jordan in a Wizards uniform? The Bulls had done nothing but struggle since Jordan, his most important teammates and his coach left a few years earlier. A city that had grown accustomed to long playoff runs hadn't come close to even making the playoffs in years. I wondered what kind of reception this prodigal would receive when he returned home.

I was astonished to see the Chicago fans accept Jordan as they did. They screamed at his introduction. They screamed when he touched the ball. They went ballistic when he scored. It was clear the United Center crowd remembered this champion of its past and wanted him to know his return was welcome. He may have been wearing a different uniform, but he was the most "at home" of any player on the court.

There is something special about coming home. Whether we've been on a long vacation, away at camp, or just gone for a weekend, the day we come home is a special one. There is something unique and calming about getting back to the place you belong.

Now, some of you are probably thinking, "What are you talking about? If I could find some way out of my hometown, where nothing happens, I would love to go somewhere else." But what if you couldn't take your friends or family and you had no possibility of making new friends? That tight-knit atmosphere wouldn't seem so bad, would it? We all long for a place where people accept us for who we are. That place is called home.

■ What does this passage tell us about coming home to God spiritually? Is it possible? What must happen in us?

_____

_____

_____

■ Because God is jealous, how does he react when we come home spiritually? Check the answer you think best reflects God's character.

❑ When we return to him, he accepts us back.

❑ When we return to him, he leaves us.

❑ When we return to him, he takes us back but holds the fact that we once left over our heads.

■ Have you ever come home to God? Explain that situation.

_____

_____

_____

■ Is there any area in your life today where you need to come home spiritually? Explain that situation.

_____

_____

_____

God's jealousy tells us that coming home spiritually is possible. The past few days, we have talked about our tendency to cheat on God and wander from him. We have spent some time repenting and have seen the emotions God wears on his sleeve as he longs for our return. The good news today is that a return is possible. We can come home. It means we will have to do away with some things in our lives. It means our lives will have to change. But if we will return to him, he will return to us. And just like there is no deeper hurt than being cheated on or deserted, there is no sweeter joy than restoration.

God's jealousy tells us that his love for us never fades. He may get upset with us, and he may discipline us. But as we learned earlier this week, God never grows apathetic toward us. The parable of the prodigal son shows the emotions of God the Father running toward us prodigals, welcoming us home with open arms.

Today God longs to run toward you, but you have to return. Today God longs to welcome you home, but you have to come home. Today God longs to express his love to you, but you have to receive that love. Today can be a homecoming for you.

prayer exercise:

Imagine coming home from a long trip. Feel the hugs of friends and family as they welcome you home from your journey. Now imagine coming home spiritually. Imagine God placing his arms around you and telling you, "Welcome home, child." Feel free to tell God everything in this moment. Tell him about your cheating and wandering. Ask for his forgiveness. Throw yourself on his grace. Thank him for making today a homecoming for you.

GOD IS...JEALOUS

the choice
between 2 loves

It's amazing what people are willing to watch on TV. But it's even more amazing to see what people are willing to do to be on TV. The rise of reality TV shows has given ordinary people the chance to step into extraordinary situations, and people are watching in record numbers. Whether it's watching a grandfather mastermind his way through *Survivor* or watching a girl let tarantulas crawl on her face on *Fear Factor*, the sight of real people playing life by different rules than normal makes us wonder what we would do in a reality show situation.

One popular reality show in 2002 was *The Bachelor*. In this show, a lone bachelor wove his way between 25 different women to find his soul-mate. Every week the field narrowed as the bachelor chose a select few by offering them a rose. America waited in anticipation as the number of women got smaller and smaller. The first season was so popular, producers began taking applications for "Year Two" before the first bachelor made his choice.

One thing that stunned me about *The Bachelor* is that twenty-five girls seemed more than willing to let this one guy date and kiss and spend time with each of the other girls, hoping that one day they would be the one to win his heart. Now, I could see this happening at the beginning of the relationship, but as the field got narrower and narrower, I didn't understand how the women dealt with it. I don't know about you, but I never dated anyone who allowed me to play the field like that.

The last night of the first season ended as the bachelor made his choice between two women clamoring for his love. The night before he presented the engagement ring to his woman of choice, he was kissing his other date, telling her that if he had to choose right then he would choose her. She was heartbroken the next night when she found out he had changed his mind.

Read James 4:1-12

The sad commentary about our lives as Christians is that many times we live our lives with God in the same way the bachelor lived his dating life. We clamor for God's attention when it is convenient, but on other nights or at different times, we chase after other things with the same passion and drive we came to God with the night before. James helps us understand that life with Christ should not be so hypocritical.

■ How do the words of this passage affect your view of your relationship with God?

_____

_____

_____

■ What is the biggest temptation for you to keep "dating" the world?

_____

_____

_____

■ What is God challenging you to do as a result of our study this week?

_____

_____

_____

The more serious a relationship becomes, the more commitment is necessary to maintain that relationship. Very few marriages would last if one marriage partner had to watch the other continue to date other people. There comes a point when commitment to one person is scary but necessary.

We face the same point in our lives spiritually every day. Every day, we are faced with a choice about what we will allow our hearts to chase after. Growing a relationship with God means daily committing that he is our one passion, our true love and our heart's desire.

Take some time to count the cost of committing to God today. You may have followed Christ for years, or you may be a new believer. Either way, each day brings with it a challenge of commitment. Spend some time preparing your heart for the battle of pleasures that you will face today. Ask and allow God to woo you with his love.

Continue this time of reflection today by writing a love note to God expressing the deep desires of your heart. (Yes, even guys can do this.) Let God know what you want to give up and what holes you need him to fill. Sign your name at the bottom of the letter, and then seal it and mail it to yourself. In a few days you will receive the note you wrote to God as a reminder of your commitment and what you have learned about God's jealousy this week.

GOD IS...JEALOUS

This page is designed to give you space to take notes during your "God is . . ." group session or to journal your reflections on the highlights of this week's study.

GOD IS...

FATHER

a God who cares

GOD IS...FATHER

Deuteronomy
30:11-20

a father
who teaches

■ When you picture God in your mind, what do you picture?

_____

_____

_____

_____

Read Matthew 6:5-13

People picture God in many different ways. The Bible is filled with all kinds of dramatic imagery to help us picture God. Some people think of God as a king ruling on his royal throne. Some people picture God as a lover desperately wooing his beloved to his side (as we talked about last week). Some people picture God as a deliverer, swooping in at the last minute to save his people from destruction. All of these pictures have a place in describing who God is.

Jesus used descriptive terminology when he talked about the attributes of God. When asked about who God is or how to address God, Jesus responded with the picture of Father more than any other. To talk about God, then, is to talk about him as Father.

For some, picturing God as Father is easy because the example of their own fathers set the foundation for them to see God. But sadly, not all of us are so fortunate. The picture of God as Father that Jesus used has been drastically distorted for many people by the examples of their earthly fathers. Few people today can talk about their fathers as their heroes. The rising rates of divorce and abandonment has led many to despise their fathers. This disturbing scenario has led to distortions in the way many people see God. But the truth remains that Jesus described God as Father.

104 Following God — God Is...

So what do we mean when we talk about God as Father? This is the question we hope this week's lesson will answer. For some of you, this picture will stretch your imagination, as you will have to trust that God is not exactly like your human father. For others, the picture your human father has set for you will illuminate who God is.

There are many different ways God acts as our Father. This week, we will think about a few of them: teaching, protecting, disciplining, supporting and providing. Like the perfect earthly dad, God fathers his children.

■ List three teachers or coaches who have impacted your life the most. Beside each name, explain how that person has impacted you.

1. _____

2. _____

3. _____

Teachers have a major impact on us. Whether we like it or not, those we listen to affect the way we think and process life. Some of the people who have most impacted my life were my teachers. My Sunday School teacher, Mr. Jim, invested his life in me, teaching me how to know God as a youngster. Coach Arrich taught me how to play soccer and how to understand physics. Dr. Goodman, Dr. Myers, and Dr. Smith challenged my perceptions of life and reality in college and seminary. As teachers, they invested their lives in helping me see clearly and understand fully how life operates.

But the teacher who invested the most in me is one I never had for a class. That teacher is my dad. My dad taught me to play soccer when I was young. My dad taught me how to tie my shoes. My dad helped me do my homework when I couldn't understand it. My dad taught me about God in principle and in my real life. Even now, I call my dad for advice.

One way that God acts as our Father is by teaching us what is right and what is wrong. In this passage of Scripture, Moses encourages the people of Israel to follow the instruction of God.

Read Deuteronomy 30:11-20

Fill in the blanks:

Deuteronomy 30:16 says, "For I command you today to _____ the Lord _____ God, to _____ in his _____, and to _____ his commands, decrees and laws."

■ According to verse 18, where does failing to follow God's instruction lead?

_____

■ Does following God's instruction mean we will always have the nicest and newest stuff and get whatever we want? Why or why not?

_____

_____

_____

God longs to teach his people. As the Creator of life, he knows what life was intended for and how it is to be lived to its fullest. But just as it's sometimes hard to trust that our parents know what is best for us, it's also sometimes hard for us to trust God. However, the truth of Deuteronomy 30 is still true today: we can trust the great Teacher who is also God, our Father.

prayer exercise:

Spend some time evaluating your picture of God as Father. How is God like your earthly Father? How is God unlike your earthly Father? If you live without your Father, how has your mother, grandparent, or guardian modeled what a Father is supposed to be? How is God the same as and different than all of these pictures? Spend the rest of today's time asking God to give you a teachable spirit, conforming your will to his will.

a father
who protects

I love to watch TV. There are few things in life I enjoy more than sitting down in front of the TV set with a cold glass of Coke and a bag of potato chips. Some of you might think that's not spiritual, but it's something I love to do. It's relaxing to channel-surf. I think my love for TV exists because, when I was a kid, my family never had cable. My dad was a bit old-fashioned and didn't want to spend the money for cable, so we spent days and nights trying to tune in ABC or NBC with rabbit-ear antennas.

Now that I'm on my own, I don't know how I lived all those years without cable. Some of you probably can't imagine life without it either. With cable, there are so many choices. Each new station provides a new option. Gone are the days of having only three networks to choose from. Now we can tune into a variety of shows with just a click of the remote. One channel I love to watch from time to time is the Discovery Channel. I'm fascinated with nature shows. I always stop to watch programs that show incredible natural disasters such as tornadoes and hurricanes up close.

After living in Florida and Alabama for a large part of my life, I know what it's like to live under a tornado warning or to go to the grocery store when a hurricane is coming. When you watch these shows on TV, they show you up close just how devastating these storms can be.

■ What is the biggest storm that you have ever seen?

_____

_____

_____

■ How did it make you feel?
- ☐ excited
- ☐ scared
- ☐ panicky
- ☐ awestruck
- ☐ fascinated
- ☐ joyful

It's one thing to watch a storm on TV but another to be caught in a storm in real life. I'll never forget a trip I took to Miami to play a soccer game my freshman year in college. It was a month or so after Hurricane Andrew had struck, and the area was devastated. Piles of branches, limbs and trees lined the streets, stacked higher than you could see over. Garbage was everywhere. You could instantly tell many lives had been torn apart. If you've watched a storm special on TV, you know what I'm talking about. To this day many of the trees in Miami are barren and look like posts sticking out of the ground.

I own an umbrella. It's not the greatest umbrella in the world, but it does the job. It's easy to travel with, and it's black, so it matches everything. It even has this neat button that makes it pop out. There are many days I'm grateful for my umbrella.

Now imagine a tornado or hurricane was coming. I love my umbrella, but in the midst of one of those storms, it wouldn't be much help. Can you imagine someone standing in the street yelling, "Bring it on, Hurricane Andrew! I'm ready for you. Don't mess with me. I've got an umbrella." A storm that powerful wouldn't be slowed at all by a little, black, nylon umbrella. In fact, if someone tried to take on one of those storms with an umbrella, we would call him a fool.

What we're looking for in these storms is a shelter, a place of safety, a place worthy of our trust. If you've ever been caught in the middle of one of these storms, you know that when they come, people go running for cover. They want a shelter, because a shelter is a place of safety and security. It's a place of protection. In these crisis moments, an umbrella, no matter how good it might be, is of little value. However, everyone who values their lives will seek shelter.

Read Psalm 27:1-6

■ What kind of storms is David facing in Psalm 27?

_____

_____

_____

_____

■ Where does David find shelter, according to verses 4-5?

_____

_____

_____

■ How has God provided shelter for you in the past?

_____

_____

_____

■ Where do you need God to provide shelter for you now?

_____

_____

_____

In Psalm 27, David's life is full of confusion. He is running from enemies who want to kill him. Being hunted is a stressful experience. But in one moment, David experiences the protection of coming into the shelter of his heavenly Father.

Notice that David doesn't think that he can handle his situation on his own. He knows that attacking life on his own is like taking on a hurricane with an umbrella. He knows what he needs is something bigger than himself, so he runs to his shelter. He goes "to gaze upon the beauty of the Lord."

I love that thought. When the world crashes down around us, God our heavenly Father is our shelter, protecting us even in our darkest nights.

Lift your anxiety to God your great protector today. Ask God to be the shelter you run to in the middle of the storms of life. Now run under that shelter. Bask in the knowledge that God your Father knows what you can bear and holds you safely in his arms.

GOD IS...FATHER

a father
who disciplines

I'll never forget one particular day from my time in nursery school—the first day I ever received a paddling. I was scared to death.

The day started out like any other at the nursery where my friends and I went each day while our parents worked. We played games, made projects and enjoyed recess. But toward the end of recess that day, a thought came across my mind that my friends and I ended up paying for in a big way.

It seemed innocent enough in the beginning. We were riding our tricycles around the outside of the nursery. But it had rained just before we came out for recess, and right off the tricycle track stood one of the greatest things I had ever seen: a huge mud puddle.

Like all little boys who love playing outside, I saw the mud puddle as a source of hours and hours of fun. So without thinking, my friends and I spent the next 30 minutes riding through the puddle. We were having the time of our lives, at least until the head nursery leader, Miss P., saw what was happening. Suddenly, all of us were pulled inside and asked what we were thinking that made us do such a terrible thing. When we couldn't come up with a suitable response, we had to line up to pay for the grievous sins we had just committed.

The fear that entered my body didn't come just from the pain I knew was coming with the paddling. I also dreaded the even harsher reality of what would happen at home after I arrived with a note pinned to my shirt saying I had received a paddling that day at school.

Discipline at my house was no laughing matter. My brother and I hated getting spanked, and we tried everything to get out of it. We put socks and books in the back of our pants. We tried to make my dad laugh so he couldn't concentrate on the spanking. We tried begging and pleading for our lives. We tried conniving by bringing in a piece of firewood when we were asked to cut down a switch for a spanking. Still, the end result was that, from time to time, discipline and pain were a necessary part of our growing experience, because the only way out we never seemed to try was doing the right thing.

■ What was your most memorable experience of being disciplined?

_____

_____

_____

Today, fewer and fewer people are spanking their children. Some of you should be extremely grateful for that. But other forms of discipline have taken the place of corporal punishment. Those of you who are grounded or on restriction right now know that too well.

No matter how your parents discipline you, every parent knows that pain is sometimes necessary to teach us lessons we will never forget.

Read Hebrews 12:1-13

Fill in the blanks:
Hebrews 12:5 says, "My son, do not make _____ of the Lord's _____, and do not lose heart when he _____ you, because the Lord _____ those he _____, and he _____ everyone he accepts as a _____. "

■ What does this passage say God's motivation for discipline is?

_____

_____

_____

■ What is our heavenly Father's goal when he disciplines us, according to verses 10-11?

_____

_____

It would be great if we never had to learn anything through discipline, if we always did the right thing and took God at his word. But the truth is that, just as we have a problem submitting to the will of our earthly parents, we have a problem submitting to and obeying our heavenly Father. When we will not listen, God gets our attention.

Sometimes he does this by formally disciplining us. Other times he allows us to go down our own roads and suffer the consequences of our actions. But as our Father, his hand of love is a hand of discipline as he guides us down life's road and makes us more like himself.

■ Describe a time when God has disciplined you in the past.

_____

_____

_____

■ What do you think God was teaching you during this time?

_____

_____

_____

prayer exercise:

Practice submission in your prayer time today by laying down your agenda for the day and picking up God's agenda. With every decision today, ask God what he wants. Spend some time practically serving your parents, teachers, friends and even your brothers and sisters. Get creative in your prayer time today by planning how you can carry out these acts of service to God, demonstrating that his will is more important than your own will today.

GOD IS...FATHER

a father
who is a cheerleader

Everyone wants to know they have someone in their corner who is fighting with them to the bitter end, pulling for them at all costs and believing in them even when things don't look good. We call these people cheerleaders or fans. Every team has them, even those teams that are not that good. Not long ago I went to a college football game between the South Carolina Gamecocks and the Georgia Bulldogs. The game was at Williams-Brice Stadium in Columbia, S.C., and 86,000 people, most of them Gamecock fans, were screaming their lungs out to cheer for their team.

I was amazed to see such passion and enthusiasm for a team that, at the time, had won just two of its last twenty-three games. Despite that lousy record, the fans were there, decked out in garnet and black, to scream their support for their team. And when South Carolina pulled off an upset victory, those fans celebrated by rushing the field and tearing down the goalposts.

My biggest fan is my dad. Every time I played a soccer game, he was there, or he called to ask me about it on the phone afterward. He knew when I was playing, and I knew without a doubt that he was on my side. He got off early from work to watch me play. He traveled hundreds of miles to see my games. He studied a sport he had had no real interest in until I started playing. And he yelled his lungs out encouraging me and my teammates to play our best.

Sometimes in the middle of games, I would look up to see if he was there. It took only a moment to see that he was. His presence was one of the most calming things I have ever known as an athlete. I knew that after the game, whether I won or lost, he would be there for me.

Read Joshua 1:1-9

Fill in the blanks:

In Joshua 1:9, God tells Joshua, "Have I not _____ you? Be _____ and _____. Do not be _____; do not be _____, for the Lord your God _____ be _____ you _____ you _____."

■ Why do you think it was important for God to let Joshua know he was in his corner?

_____

_____

_____

■ How do you think it helped Joshua to know God was with him?

_____

_____

_____

From this passage, we might conclude that Joshua had a confidence problem, because three times God tells Joshua to "Be strong and courageous." But think about where Joshua's strength and courage came from. One little phrase sums it up: "For I am with you." God is saying to Joshua, "I know the task I have called you to seems bigger than you. I know you don't have too much confidence in your own talents and abilities. But Joshua, just like I was with Moses, I will be with you. Joshua, I am your biggest fan." Joshua had to be encouraged by that statement from God.

We all need cheerleaders. As Christians, God has given us the same promise he gave Joshua. Throughout the Bible, God is shown to be a God who stands with his people. He is not distant, as we learned when we studied how God is personal. He looks after his children and fights and cheers for his sons and daughters.

■ What hope do you get from knowing that, because God is your Father, he takes your side and cheers for you as a Christian?

_____

_____

_____

■ Write down an experience when you felt as though someone was in your corner. Explain that situation.

_____

_____

_____

_____

_____

■ How does this experience give you a better picture of God as your Father?

_____

_____

_____

_____

_____

prayer exercise:

If you can today, go to some sort of game or activity or watch one on TV. Instead of just talking with friends, cheer hard for your favorite team. As you cheer, let the truth in today's devotion sink into your life. Allow God to pound into your heart the truth that he is with you, cheering for you, fighting through life with you.

a father
who provides

Matthew 7:7-12

My wife loves birds. When we lived in Birmingham, Alabama, we had two bird feeders that hung right outside the sliding glass doors on our balcony. Every day, birds came from all over the place to these feeders to eat the food my wife had provided for them. We had all kinds of birds at our bird feeders: doves, cardinals, blue jays, and even hummingbirds that came to a feeder designed especially for them.

My wife would sit for hours just watching the birds. One Christmas, my wife's grandmother gave her some binoculars and a book to identify different species of birds so she could see the birds up close and figure out what kinds were coming to our feeders. Like the perfect guardian, my wife carefully stocked and restocked the bird feeder, washed out the bird bath and did all the little things someone who loves birds does.

I must admit that I'm not a bird lover. I sometimes got annoyed with the commotion and mess birds made on our balcony. I would rather watch TV than watch birds. Whenever I had to do the bird-related chores my wife loved to do, I began to get a little perturbed with the birds that were just waiting for me to feed them.

> ## Read Matthew 7:7-12; 10:23-31

Fill in the blanks:
Complete the following phrases from Matthew 7:7-8:

Ask and _____

Seek and you _____

Knock and the door _____

■ What do these passages teach us about our responsibility as we come to God with our needs?

_____

_____

_____

■ Does Matthew 7:7-12 teach that God will give us whatever we want as long as we ask for it?

❑ yes
❑ no

Explain your answer.

_____

_____

_____

_____

■ Compare and contrast these verses with Matthew 6:25-33, a passage you studied a few weeks ago.

_____

_____

_____

_____

As I read a passage of Scripture not long ago, the thought of how God is our provider gripped my heart like never before. Martin Luther said, "Scripture has hands and feet. It runs after a man, it grips him." This is what happened to me as I watched my wife spend precious time caring for the birds that randomly came across our balcony looking for a free meal.

As I watched her care for the birds, I was thankful that our God is not like me. I couldn't care less whether the birds at our balcony ate or not. Yet even more than my wife looked after the birds that came to our balcony, our heavenly Father looks after all creation. And as human beings, we stand as the supreme creation of God, because we are made in his image. Matthew's message is that God looks after us as a good provider, giving us what we need and watching to make sure we are all right.

Spend the day in silent prayer as you go about your normal routine. As you go through the day, notice the little ways in which God is providing for his creation. The grass is growing; the birds are eating; rain is falling; and the sun is shining. Let these things remind you of how God our Father provides for us in so many ways. Thank him as you walk through your day for the little things he does every day throughout our lives. He is a good God, and he gives us more to be thankful for than we even know.

This page is designed to give you space to take notes during your "God is . . ." group session or to journal your reflections on the highlights of this week's study.

GOD IS...

ORDINARY

a God who became
one of us

GOD IS... ORDINARY

God in the everyday

Many of us fall into the trap of looking for God in miraculous signs. We want to see a burning bush or a parted sea. It's easy for us to spend our lives looking for God in miraculous things while we miss his presence right beside us the whole time. We often overlook daily reminders of his presence.

This week, we're going to focus on how God is ordinary, working in and around us all the time.

I hate it when I lose my keys or my wallet. It's a miserable experience. I'm sure you've done it before. You misplace your keys and then spend forever trying to find them.

One time, I had an appointment to meet someone for lunch. When I went to get my keys, I couldn't find them. After looking everywhere, I ended up having to call the restaurant to ask someone there to tell my friend that I wouldn't be there because I couldn't find my car keys. I was embarrassed.

I looked for my keys for more than two hours. When my wife came home from work, I told her about my ordeal. She said, "I think your keys are on the key hook." Sure enough, I went to the place where we kept keys, and mine were hanging there. They had been in the most obvious place the entire time, yet I had missed them. I was looking everywhere but in the most obvious place.

■ Do you ever think you have missed God by looking for him in miraculous signs instead of everyday, normal places?

❏ yes
❏ no

■ Why do you think people tend to gravitate toward seeing God only in the extraordinary?

_____

_____

_____

■ List three places that remind you of God's presence.

1. _____

2. _____

3. _____

Read Romans 1:20

In this verse, we learn that God has always been available to be known through the things he has made. Think back to the beginning of time. Who made the trees? Who made the waters? Who made the stars, the sky, the moon, the sun and the galaxies? All of these things point us toward our heavenly Father.

One time I was speaking at a camp in the mountains. I had a few free hours, so I decided to go for a walk. I started walking without knowing where I would end up. After about thirty minutes, I came upon a rock that overlooked miles and miles of beautiful land. As I stood there, all I could think about was God. His voice did not come to me in loud thunder. I did not see rainbows, nor was I visited by angels. I simply stood in awe of the God who had created all that I saw. What marvelous things he has made!

■ Has God ever revealed himself to you through nature? When was the last time he did this?

_____

_____

_____

_____

_____

_____

■ Have you ever taken the time to take a walk or sit on the beach and think about the ordinary awesomeness of our God? What was that experience like?

_____

_____

_____

■ What are some things you could do to allow God to help you see him in the ordinary?

_____

_____

_____

prayer exercise:

Take a walk outside for at least thirty minutes. During your walk, ask God to show himself to you in some ordinary way. He might teach you a lesson about himself through a bird, a tree, a stream, or a sunset. Expect him to answer your prayer.

GOD IS... ORDINARY

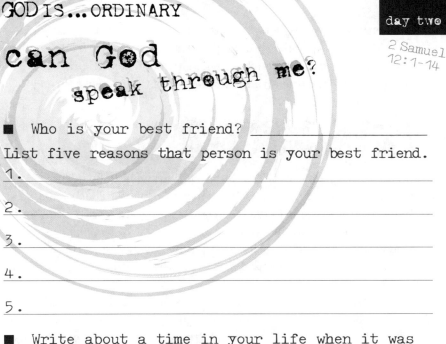

day two

2 Samuel
12:1-14

can God speak through me?

■ Who is your best friend? _____

List five reasons that person is your best friend.

1. _____

2. _____

3. _____

4. _____

5. _____

■ Write about a time in your life when it was obvious God was speaking directly to you through a friend.

_____

_____

_____

When I was sixteen years old, I felt as though God was calling me to do something. Though I couldn't quite put my finger on it, I was pretty sure he was calling me into full-time Christian ministry. It was an exciting but confusing time. I prayed and prayed but couldn't nail down exactly what God was calling me to do.

I was extremely fortunate because I had a group of solid Christian friends with whom I shared about my potential call to ministry. I asked my friends question after question to see what they thought about the situation.

I did not realize it at the time, but God spoke to me through three particular friends who confirmed my call to ministry. Their affirmation was nothing miraculous or earth-shattering. It was just a few friends who confirmed things about me as a person and about my future.

Fourteen years later, as I look back on that experience, I know without a doubt that God spoke to me through those friends. He confirmed my call to ministry through people who were walking through life with me. It is pretty amazing to me that an almighty God sometimes speaks through ordinary people like us.

Read 2 Samuel 12:1-14

God uses other people to tell us things we don't want to hear. This passage sets the scene right after David had an affair with Bathsheba. Nathan the prophet came to see David and shared a story with him about a greedy man who took what was not his.

David was furious and made it clear that the greedy man in the story was in the wrong. Little did he know that Nathan was painting the picture of what David had done.

God used Nathan to reveal the sin David was in and to invite David to change. It's neat how God does that. Throughout the Bible, God uses people to convey his truth to others. God speaks through ordinary human beings.

■ Has God ever used you to speak to another person? Explain that situation.

_____

_____

_____

■ Is there anyone in your life who needs some Godly affirmation? Ask the Father to place someone on your mind to whom you can speak a word of encouragement. Who is that person? What kind of encouragement does this person need?

_____

_____

_____

■ Perhaps you identify with Nathan and say that you know someone who is in the wrong and needs to hear truth from God's perspective. Is there a David in your life whom you need to talk to in love?

    ❑ yes
    ❑ no

Who? _____

If we are not careful, we will miss wonderful opportunities to hear God speak to us because we are always looking for the extraordinary. Sometimes God speaks through a family member, friend, or teacher. If our desire is to follow God and listen to his voice, we need to ask him to help us recognize those times when he is speaking to us through the people around us. It is important to surround yourself with godly friends and wise counsel, because God speaks to us through others.

■ List three people who are pursuing God whom you could see God using to speak to you about a decision you may be facing. Choose people who are in your circle.

1. _____

2. _____

3. _____

Is there anything better than having a good group of friends? We were not meant to live life alone. God intends for all of us to have a solid community of brothers and sisters so that we can help each other on our journeys with him.

Ask God to help you listen to him when he speaks through your godly friends or family members. Share with God your desire to be a person who listens to his voice. Praise him for being a God who speaks to us in the ordinary.

GOD IS... ORDINARY

a loud
silence

Many of us love to go to ballgames where the crowds are big and noisy. We pride ourselves on being the loudest fans for our favorite team. People flock to concerts to enjoy the ear-blasting music that comes from oversized speakers. Regular car stereos are not loud enough, so we get special systems put into our cars to play music at a volume that someone three states away can hear. We love noise.

How many times have you been studying and turned on the radio for background music? People turn on their television sets, even though they are not watching, so there will be noise in the room. Why are we so afraid of silence?

It might be because silence can be deafening. We are a culture addicted to adrenaline-fed spirituality. But when we study our church fathers and great women of the faith from yesteryear, we see that all of them knew the power of silence before God. Could there be power in silence?

■ When was the last time that you spent more than thirty minutes by yourself in complete silence—where you said absolutely nothing?

- ❏ yesterday
- ❏ last week
- ❏ last month
- ❏ last year
- ❏ years ago
- ❏ never

■ Do you think it is important to spend time in silence during your week? Why or why not?

_____

_____

_____

Fill in the blanks:

Mark 1:35 says, "Very _____ in the
_____, while it was still dark, Jesus
_____ _____, _____ the house
and _____ off to a _____
_____, where he _____."

Jesus is our supreme example of how to live the Christian life. We are his apprentices on this journey with God. As we look at his life, we see him at various times retreating to solitary and quiet places. Why does Jesus do this? Why was the Son of God drawn to places of silence?

In this verse, we see Jesus getting up early and heading off to a quiet place to pray. Jesus knew the power of solitude. He knew that the best times with his heavenly Father came in solitude and silence. No distractions. No noise. No company. It was just Jesus and his Father.

■   Why do you think Jesus made it a priority to spend time with God in solitary and silent places?

_____

_____

_____

I was speaking at a retreat in Georgia one weekend and had a hard time sleeping. So early in the morning, I got out of bed and walked down to the lake. It was so calm and quiet. There wasn't a ripple in the water. Everything was still and peaceful.

I stood there taking everything in. Like most guys do, I started throwing rocks into the lake. I tried to find the biggest rocks possible. After a little while had passed, I started to notice something. The ripples from the splashes of the rocks made their way all the way back to the shore where I stood.

I did not think much about that until I went back to the lake later that afternoon with others. We were skiing and swimming, the wind was blowing and the water was rough. Guys were doing what guys do, throwing big rocks into the lake. This time, however, things were different. You could hardly even see the rocks splash because the water was so rough.

There was a big difference in the lake between the morning and the afternoon. When the water was quiet and still, you could see the splash and then the ripples. When the water was rough and busy, you could hardly even notice a rock going into the water.

When we are still and quiet, we are in a position to hear God more clearly than when our lives are full of noise and busyness. God reveals himself in quiet moments. We have to fight our culture's tendency to have noise around us all of the time. We have to be a people who are committed to finding times of quiet and solitude with God.

■　Will you commit to spending time in silence before God on a regular basis?

   ❏ yes
   ❏ no

■　List three ways you can start incorporating times of silence with God into your life.

1. _____

2. _____

3. _____

prayer exercise:

Go to a place where you can hear absolutely nothing. For twenty minutes, sit in complete silence. Before you begin, ask God to speak to you. After that, don't say a word. Listen to the silence. It can be extremely loud. This may be a little difficult for you to do at first, but if you practice and stick with it, you will find it extremely beneficial.

speaking through
circumstance

■ Has God ever spoken to you through a circumstance in your life, or do you know of anyone to whom God spoke through circumstance? Explain that situation.

_____

_____

_____

■ List some examples from the Bible when God spoke through an event in someone's life.

_____

_____

_____

When I graduated from high school, I had the desire to go to a particular college. I would lay in my bed at night and dream about what it would be like to be a student at this big university. I love to go to sporting events, and this school offered endless opportunities for that. I could hardly wait.

But there was one problem. As I prayed to God about where I should go to school, I kept getting the feeling that he did not want me to attend this particular school. I wanted this more than anything in the world, but I kept seeing red flags from God. I talked to my parents and friends about it, and I kept hearing the same thing. It was really frustrating.

As I continued to pray, God made it clear to me that he was leading me to a local junior college. I was so mad. I wanted to move away from home and live on my own, but I knew it was not what I needed to do. His plans were not my plans. I was frustrated and angry with God. I enrolled at this junior college, but I went kicking and screaming. I had the worst attitude.

What happened over the next two years at that school was probably the best thing that could have happened to me. I built life-long friendships, grew with God, and experienced a place of community that I have yet to see again. I had such a great time there that, had it been a four-year school, I would have stayed. After I finished at the junior college, I ended up transferring to the university I originally wanted to attend. I had a blast there, but I also know that if I had started off there, I probably would not have made it through my first semester.

God knows what he is doing. As I look back on it now, I can clearly see he spoke to me through this experience in my life. Once again, there was no thunder or lightning. It was God in the ordinary speaking to me.

■ Have you ever wondered why you were going through something only to later look back on it and see the hand of God in your life? Explain that situation.

_____

_____

_____

■ Why do you think God speaks to us through circumstances?

_____

_____

_____

Read Genesis 37

Genesis 37 contains an amazing story. What did Joseph do to deserve this kind of treatment? He did not ask to have these dreams. He was not being a bad person. He told the truth to his brothers and his father, and look what he got in return. He was sold into slavery.

Can you imagine what was going through his mind? I would have been so mad if I were him. I try to picture myself at the bottom of that well in the desert. What kind of questions would I be asking God? I think I would say something like, "Thanks a lot, God. What did I do to deserve this? I thought you cared about me."

I couldn't blame Joseph if he felt this way. But if you continue to read the story in Genesis, you will find that things come full circle with Joseph and his brothers. God had a plan for Joseph throughout his entire ordeal, speaking and revealing himself the whole time. Joseph may not have realized that until a great while later, but God was speaking and working. What his brothers had meant for evil, God meant for good.

■   Have you ever had to trust that God was working or speaking to you in a circumstance even though you could not see him? Explain that situation.

_____

_____

prayer exercise:

Trusting God in the midst of our circumstances is a daily thing. Ask God to help you realize the truth that he speaks to you in ordinary ways through your circumstances even though you may not see it at first. Ask him for the strength to trust when it is difficult to do so.

GOD IS... ORDINARY

why
church?

■ Why do you go to church? Check all that apply. Be honest with yourself.

❏ I want to worship God corporately.
❏ I feel like I should.
❏ My parents make me.
❏ I want to see my friends.
❏ Life was never meant to be lived alone.
❏ I want to make God happy.
❏ I want to check it off my list.

■ What is the purpose of church?

_____

_____

_____

■ Regardless of why you go to church, does God ever speak or reveal Himself to you at church?

❏ yes
❏ no

If your answer is yes, how?

_____

_____

_____

Read the following quote from Philip Yancey's book, *Church: Why Bother?* and spend a few minutes thinking through it. Let these words sink deeply into you and see if you can relate to what the author is saying.

Christianity is not a purely intellectual, internal faith. It can only be lived in community. Perhaps for this reason, I have never entirely given up on church. At a deep level I sense that church contains something I desperately need. Whenever I abandon church for a time, I find that I am the one who suffers. My faith fades, and the crusty shell of lovelessness grows over me again. I grow colder rather that hotter. And so my journeys away from church have always circled back inside.

(Philip Yancey, *Church: Why Bother?*
[Grand Rapids, Michigan: Zondervan Publishing House, 2001], 32)

I will never forget the time when I was in the tenth grade and a friend of mine asked me this question, "Why do you go to church?" I gave some Sunday School answer and went on with my day. But that question haunted me for a very long time. I spent a lot of time answering that question for myself over the next few years. Why did I go to church? Why do I go to church now?

Read Acts 2:42-47

Fill in the blanks:

Acts 2:42 says, "They _____ themselves to the apostles' _____ and to the _____, to the _____ of _____ and to _____."

This is one of the most amazing passages in the entire Bible. It is a picture of the early church. Do you notice that the people of the church were together learning, sharing, giving, and living? We can't miss this. God speaks to us through each other. We are the church. This is one of the simplest yet most powerful truths in the world.

When we pray together (v. 42), God speaks. When we share (v. 45), God speaks. When we go to worship together on Sundays or during the week, God is there. Where two or more are gathered in his name, he is there.

As we search through how God is in the ordinary, this is a key. We were never meant to do life alone. We were made for community. Nowadays, many people would rather go on a hunt for the miraculous signs of God than simply meet, pray, preach, share, and cry together. Church is about community. Church is about a group of people worshiping and praising God together. Church is about people helping each other become more like Christ. That's what the body of Christ is all about, and the community of the church offers it.

- What do you like about your church? Why do you like those things?

_____

_____

_____

- If you could change something about your church, what would it be? Why?

_____

_____

_____

- Why do you think community is so important?

_____

_____

Jesse Ventura, ex-governor of Minnesota, former Navy SEAL and professional wrestler, once said that organized religion is a sham and a crutch for weak people. Jesus sees things a little differently. As Christians, we know that we need each other. God dwells in our midst, ordinary but powerful. The next time you go to church, remember this about God. Church is where believers walk with one another on their journey toward home. We hear and see God act as we walk together.

prayer exercise:

Praise God for the church. Ask him to forgive you when you complain about little things inside the church. Ask God to help you see the big picture of community and his presence inside of the church.

GOD IS...ORDINARY

_____

_____

_____

_____

_____

_____

_____

_____

_____

_____

_____

_____

_____

This page is designed to give you space to take notes during your "God is . . ." group session or to journal your reflections on the highlights of this week's study.

GOD IS...

MYSTERIOUS

a God of
so much more

GOD IS... MYSTERIOUS

can't figure
him out

I love a good mystery movie. I like it when I can't figure out the ending of a movie until it happens. You think you know who the bad guy is, but do you really know? You're trying to figure it out as the plot unravels.

There's something about mystery that draws us in. Perhaps we like things that challenge us. In some weird way, we like not being able to figure something or someone out. We're attracted to movie characters or real people who are "mysterious." We like things that are unpredictable.

When I was growing up, people around me in the church talked about God in exact and very predictable terms. It seemed as though they had him all figured out. Everything seemed so simple and easy to explain. But as I have grown up in my faith, I have realized that God is the most mysterious being in the history of the universe. Just when you think you have him figured out, he blows your mind.

God is mysterious. We need to be reminded of this truth. When we contemplate and meditate on his mysteriousness, it draws us into a deeper and more meaningful worship of who he is.

Even though we understand more about God than we did when we began this study, we're nowhere close to knowing fully who God is. That's the truth we'll focus on this week. We will never completely figure our mysterious God out, and that's the way it should be.

■ How would you describe the mysteriousness of God?

_____

_____

_____

_____

_____

_____

■ Has there ever been a time in your life where God just blew your mind? Explain that situation

_____

_____

_____

_____

_____

We're going to start this devotion by doing something strange. Open your Bible and turn to Genesis 1:1.

Read Genesis 1:1

Focus on the first four words.

Fill in the blanks:

Genesis 1:1 begins, "_____ _____ _____,
_____."

Now close your Bible.

prayer exercise:

After you have read those four words and have closed your Bible, close your eyes. Spend the next ten minutes reflecting on those words. Don't say a word. Sit in silence and let these words sink into you. "In the beginning God." Meditate on the mystery present in those words.

In Week One, we addressed the enormity of God. He shatters all paradigms. Where did God come from? Has he always been here? Who created God? Has there ever been a moment when God did not exist? These are some unbelievable questions. The first four words of the Bible are remarkable. "In the beginning God." Think about how mysterious our God is.

There has never been a time when God has not been here. God has always been. He is the Alpha and the Omega, the beginning and the end. Sometimes it is beneficial to sit and contemplate the hugeness of the mystery of God. He can't be figured out. He can't be placed in a box. He can't be manipulated. He does what he pleases. He makes the sun come up and down and causes the stars to stay in place. He makes the oceans roar. Our God is wonderfully mysterious.

I have played golf all of my life. I started playing competitively at a very early age. It was all I knew for so long. I loved going to the course and hitting ball after ball after ball. I enjoyed the rush of adrenaline that came when I played in tournaments.

But something strange happened to me when I played golf in college. I went to my coach one day and said something that completely shocked him. I told him, "I've lost the desire to play the game." I really meant it. I was so accustomed to it and used to it being an everyday activity that I just lost all desire to play. It took four years for me to have any desire to play again. But now I enjoy it more than I ever did before.

We have lost a sense of the mystery of God. We get so used to Sunday School answers about him that we fall into the trap of thinking we have him figured out. We are so systematic in the way we follow Him. We have lost a sense of his great and deep mysteriousness, and we need to rediscover it.

 Have you lost a sense of God's mysteriousness? Why or why not?

_____

_____

_____

_____

■ How does the mystery of God draw us into
deeper worship of who he is?

_____

_____

_____

_____

prayer exercise:

Praise God for his mystery. Ask him
to help you always walk through life
with a sense of his mysteriousness.

when it
doesn't make sense

■ Has there ever been a time in your life when God did not make sense to you? Explain that situation.

_____

_____

_____

■ What are we supposed to do when God does not make sense to us?

_____

_____

_____

I don't like to fly in airplanes. I never have, and I never will. But I have to fly quite often for my job or to visit friends. As I approach the airport, my stomach starts to turn. I get a little nervous and try to tell myself to calm down. Sometimes that works, but sometimes it doesn't.

As I walk through the airport, I try to figure out a way to get out of flying. Invariably, though, I have to get on the plane, because it's too late to drive from my home in South Carolina to Louisiana or Texas or wherever I'm going.

One of the reasons I don't like flying is that it doesn't make sense to me. I will never understand how something as heavy as a jet can get into the air. I know there are aerodynamics at work, but I don't understand them. All I know is that a plane is heavy, and I have no idea how it flies.

However, even though I don't understand how a plane flies and probably never will, I still fly. I have learned to trust the airplane. I'm actually becoming a calmer passenger. There have even been a few times recently when I was completely fine with flying. I just have to trust the airplane and the pilots. Either I do that, or I choose not to fly. It's that simple.

Sometimes trusting God is difficult. He does not always make sense to us. He can be very confusing and unpredictable at times. But if there is anything that I have learned in my journey with God, it is that sometimes you have to trust when you don't know how to trust. The decision comes down to this: If I don't trust God, where else can I turn? Sometimes you just have to make the choice to trust God and God alone.

Read John 6:60-68

I love how the Bible portrays Peter. I think many of us can relate to him. In this passage, Jesus had just finished telling a group of people that true life comes through his flesh and his flesh only. Jesus was saying that true life came exclusively through him.

This was a tough teaching for this group of people, and some turned away and left. Jesus then asked his disciples if they wanted to leave also. Peter spoke up and said, "To whom else shall we go? You have the words of eternal life."

There are times in the Bible where Jesus says some difficult things. This is one example. The disciples probably did not completely understand what Jesus was talking about. They were likely a little confused. But Peter's answer is a beautiful one that we should take to heart. Where else are we supposed to go?

Philip Yancey wrote the marvelous book, *Disappointment with God*. In this book, he tackles some tough questions about the unpredictability and mystery of God. At the end of the book, Yancey asks a poignant question: Would you rather be disappointed with God or disappointed without Him? That's a pretty bold question.

Sometimes God does not make sense. Sometimes, in his mystery, we are left scratching our heads wondering what to do. But we still have to make the choice: are we going to trust him or not?

■ Can you relate to Peter in this passage? How so?

_____

_____

_____

■ How would you answer the question Jesus posed to Peter?

_____

_____

_____

prayer exercise:

Take some time to reread this passage of scripture. Ask God to give you the courage and strength to trust him in the midst of his mysteriousness.

GOD IS...MYSTERIOUS

no box
big enough

Do you remember the Taco Bell dog? (If you are going through this study with a group, you talked about it in Week One.) For a while, this talking chihuahua was an advertising phenomenon. He walked around talking about how much he wanted Taco Bell food—"Yo quiero Taco Bell." His accent was hilarious. People loved the ads so much that Taco Bell even sold stuffed versions of the little dog for a while.

When those ads were most popular, the movie *Godzilla* came out. The movie producers teamed with Taco Bell for a joint advertising campaign. In one of the commercials, the Taco Bell chihuahua goes looking for Godzilla. The dog calls out, "Here lizard, lizard, lizard." He wants to put Godzilla in a little box he is carrying. After looking around during the entire commercial, the dog finally finds Godzilla. When he sees the "lizard" he has been chasing, the dog says, "I think I need a bigger box."

In the final week of our study, we again come to this realization. The first week of this study focused on how God is huge. As we conclude by studying God's mysteriousness, we need to see how the two are related. Because God is mysterious, He is bigger than any box in which we could ever try to place Him.

■ How does it make you feel that, after eight weeks of study, you still don't know all there is to know about God? Check all that apply.

❑ scared
❑ relieved
❑ comforted
❑ anxious
❑ overwhelmed
❑ awestruck

■ Why do you think many people tend to place God in a box and act as though they have him figured out?

_____

_____

_____

■ How has this series challenged your box?

_____

_____

_____

I love going to the ocean. I like to go into the water to swim. But when I was a little kid, I did not realize that there was a "deep end" in the ocean. I guess I thought I could stand up anywhere in the ocean. I had a rude awakening one day when the undertow dragged me out a bit. I realized very quickly that not only did the ocean have a deep end but that its deep end made the swimming pool look like a puddle.

God is like that. Just when we think we have conquered the deep end, we realize that we have only been in the kiddie pool. His waters are the deepest.

Read Psalm 104

When we read this passage, it seems silly to think that we can place God in some small box or to think we have him all figured out. After reading this psalm, my mind hurts as I try to contemplate how huge God is. He is simply amazing.

■ What are some of your reflections from this psalm?

_____

_____

_____

■ Do you tend to forget the awesome majesty and power of God? If so, why do you forget?

_____

_____

_____

I can relate to the Taco Bell dog, and it's not just because I love burritos too. I realized I need a bigger box. God does that to us. He calls us to himself and reveals himself to us. We enjoy his fellowship, and then, before we know it, we are overwhelmed by his presence. I don't want a God I can figure out. I don't want a God who fits neatly into my little box. I don't want a God who always makes sense.

When I think about God's mystery and hugeness, it draws me closer to Him. We serve and worship a God who is so much bigger than us. If you have a box, throw it away. Your God is so much bigger than that.

■ List three ways you can get rid of your box.

1. _____

2. _____

3. _____

prayer exercise:

Ask God to show you how big, mysterious, and awesome he is. Ask him to draw you into a deeper appreciation and awe of who he is.

can we
know him completely?

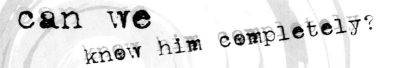

■ Is it possible to know all of who God is?

☐ yes

☐ no

Why or why not?

_____

_____

_____

■ Why will there always be more for us to know
about God?

_____

_____

_____

As a kid, I loved to go to my grandparents' house. They lived on a lake
where we could ski, swim, and fish. It was like a vacation every time I visited
them. I looked forward to those trips for weeks.

Sometimes I would take some friends to my grandparents' house. My
friends loved it there too. We would spend the whole day in the water. I
knew every inch of the cove my grandparents' dock was on. I knew where
the fish were, how deep the water was in particular places, where the
turtles liked to go and where we could dive in without worrying about it
being too shallow. Sometimes we would even take my grandparents' canoe
out for a ride, paddling all over the cove. I knew every single inch of it.

I will never forget the day my grandfather asked if I wanted to take a ride
with him on his new pontoon boat. We loaded up and headed out. My ten-
year-old mind thought we would just ride around the cove. But my

grandfather went under a bridge and made his way around an embankment. When we turned that corner, my mouth dropped. We were heading to the biggest body of water I had ever seen.

I had spent years at that lake, but I never knew how big the lake was. I had always stayed in the cove. I was shocked to find out there were miles upon miles of lake beyond the cove that I wasn't aware of. It was overwhelming and awesome.

■ Does the mystery of God enhance your daily worship?

❑ yes
❑ no

Why?

_____

_____

Read Philippians 3:10-21

Fill in the blank:
Philippians 3:10 says, "I want to _____ Christ."

We can never reach the bottom of the depths of God. He is too big and overwhelming. It makes our heads spin to think about how big he is. However, our desire should be like the one Paul expresses in this verse. Paul wanted to know Christ. He had a desire to know him as much as he possibly could. Paul knew he could never reach the bottom of the depths of God, but that did not stop him from striving to know his Savior.

There will always be part of the lake we will never get to. But in our journeys with God, we are called to search and explore his many waters. In his mystery, he is huge and beyond anything that we can comprehend. But we have the Holy Spirit to guide us as we search for God. It's an amazing concept when you think about it. This God of ours invites us to take a journey into who he is. If we take this invitation seriously, we will find new coves in these waters, and they will make us thirsty for more of him.

■ Is the cry of your heart, "I want to know Christ?" Why?

_____

_____

_____

■ Why should we seek after God even though we will never know all of him on this earth?

_____

_____

_____

prayer exercise:

Take a few moments to praise God for his mystery. Thank him for not being a God we can figure out. Praise him because, while we are here on this earth, we will never journey into all of him. Exalt him for his greatness. Continue the practice of spending some time in silence before your awesome God.

can't find
the words

■ Have you ever seen anything that left you speechless? Explain that situation. Why did it leave you speechless?

_____

_____

_____

■ What do you think causes us to lose our words when we see something breathtaking?

_____

_____

_____

My dad grew up in Georgia about twenty miles from the town of Augusta. If you are a golf fan, then you realize what happens every April in Augusta. The most prestigious golf tournament in the world, the Masters, is held there.

When my dad was growing up, they had a hard time giving away Masters tickets, so he never had a problem when he wanted to go. As a result, we have had tickets in my family for more than forty years. But now, the Masters may be the toughest sporting event ticket in the world to get. People offer as much as $20,000 for a week's worth of badges.

When I was twelve, my dad told me he was taking me to the Masters. I couldn't believe it. I grew up playing golf, and anyone who plays the game has dreamed of walking the course at Augusta National. That dream was about to come true for me.

I could not sleep the night before I went. I tossed and turned as visions of this beautiful course and the best golfers in the world playing on it raced through my head. I woke my dad up at 5:00 A.M., and we headed to Augusta.

My heart was racing as we approached the course. We showed the security guard our badges and then walked toward the first fairway. When we came through the trees, for the first time in my life I saw something that made me freeze. It was the most beautiful sight I had ever seen. I just stood there and gazed out over the course.

My dad was smiling as he said, "What do you think?" I couldn't answer him. I had no words to describe the beauty I saw in front of me. How do you describe something that you don't have words for?

■ Has God ever revealed himself to you in a way that left you speechless in light of his awesome majesty and mystery?

_____

_____

_____

Read Revelation 1:9-18

I love how John reacts in this passage. He is completely overwhelmed by Jesus. Jesus speaks to John and tells him to write about what he sees. But when John turns around to see who it is that is talking to him, he falls to the ground like a dead man. What awesome majesty! What awesome power! What awesome holiness!

It's pretty silly to think that we can put God in a box, isn't it? Just when we think that we have things under control and we have God figured out, he presents himself to us as he did to John and, in his mysteriousness, completely blows us away. It might happen through a circumstance, someone else speaking to us, the Bible, a pastor, or just a sense of the Almighty speaking directly to us. Whatever the means, the truth is that God is the greatest mystery of all time.

We will never figure him out. He takes our thoughts and shows us that we can never think enough about him. He is huge, personal, holy, gracious, jealous, our Father, ordinary, and mysterious.

We have lost a sense of the mystery of God. This is a terrible thing. God is not some self-help, "three-step-program" God. He is a God of mystery who, in his graciousness, makes himself known through his Son.

■ What does your appreciation for the mystery of God look like in your daily walk with him?

_____

_____

_____

We've learned a lot about who God is in this study, but the truth is we are still at the beginning. God's mysteriousness means that our journey with him will never grow old. There's always more we can discover and learn about who God is.

prayer exercise:

Talk to God about this passage in Revelation. Ask him to bring you to a place where you marvel at his majesty. Ask him to mold you into a person who is willing to surrender everyday to the mysterious God. Ask him to continue to lead you on a journey into who he is.

GOD IS...MYSTERIOUS

_____

_____

_____

_____

_____

_____

_____

_____

_____

_____

_____

_____

_____

_____

_____

   This page is designed to give you space to take notes during your "God is . . ." group session or to journal your reflections on the highlights of this week's study.

GOD IS...
About the Authors

DAVID RHODES has a passion to guide people in the journey of the Christian faith. He speaks at camps, conferences, retreats, and churches and also writes devotional material, camp curriculum, and D-Now material. David graduated from Palm Beach Atlantic College in 1995 and earned his Master of Divinity in 2000 from Beeson Divinity School. Since 2000, David has been on staff with Wayfarer Ministries and has been a teacher at Engage, a praise-and-worship Bible study for 20-somethings in upstate  South Carolina. David's commitment to leading people to engage their hearts, souls, minds, and hands in God is evident in his preaching, teaching, and writing. David, wife Kim, and daughter Emma, live in Moore, S.C.

CHAD NORRIS desires to lead people in their journeys to become fully devoted followers of God. He does so through speaking, teaching and  writing. After graduating from the University of Georgia in 1995, Chad received his Master of Divinity from Beeson Divinity School in 2000. While at Beeson, he also served as the college minister at The Church of Brook Hills in Birmingham, Alabama. Since 2000, Chad has been on staff with Wayfarer Ministries and has been one of the teachers for Engage, a praise-and-worship Bible study for 20-somethings in upstate South Carolina. Chad's love of "the journey" and his realistic viewpoints help nurture people in their personal spiritual growth. Chad, wife Wendy, and son Samuel, live in Spartanburg, S.C.

For more information regarding the authors of this study, please contact:

Wayfarer Ministries
Box Number 201
1735 John B. White Sr. Boulevard
Suite 9
Spartanburg, SC 29301-5462
www.wayfarerministries.org

notes

notes

notes

notes

notes

notes

notes

notes

notes